D1576188

THE
AMERICANS
WITH
DISABILITIES
ACT

A REVIEW
OF BEST
PRACTICES

Timothy L. Jones

AMA Management Briefing

AMA Membership Publications Division
American Management Association

For information on how to order additional copies of this publication, see page 123.

Library of Congress Cataloging-in-Publication Data

Jones, Timothy L.
  The Americans with Disabilities Act : a review of best practices /
  Timothy L. Jones.
    p.   cm. — (AMA management briefing)
  ISBN 0-8144-2350-7 : $10.00
    1. Handicapped—Employment—United States. 2. Handicapped–
  –Employment—Law and legislation—United States. 3. Handicapped–
  –Legal status, laws, etc.—United States. 4. Discrimination in
  employment—Law and legislation—United States. 5. United States.
  Americans with Disabilities Act of 1990. I. Title. II. Series.
  HD7256.U5J66   1993
  331.5'9—dc20   *92-38227*
                                                          CIP

The mention of products by brand name in this publication is for purposes of information only. No endorsement by the American Management Association is intended or implied.

This Management Briefing has been distributed to all U.S. members enrolled in the American Management Association.

First printing.

Contents

Acknowledgments

To my wife and children, who with grace and patience endured both my absence and my absentmindedness while I wrote; to Beverly Floyd, Debbie Evans, and Bill Tarbett, who with quiet diligence and perseverance typed parts of the manuscript and more importantly, maintained the company while I was lost in thought; to Pamela Werntz, Maggie Leedy, Don Bohl, Paul Hearn, and Anne Deschamps, who with wisdom and insight reviewed drafts of the text and offered the comments that created the book's good parts (I take responsibility for the rest); to friends and family, who with kindness and enthusiasm encouraged me at the right time and in the right way; and to those who with understanding and integrity taught me what I know about employing people with disabilities; to all of you, I offer sincere and humble thanks.

Introduction

For many companies, the very idea of emulating "best practices" under the Americans with Disabilities Act (ADA) may seem daunting. Given the uncertainty that most managers feel, having confidence that *any* practice meets ADA's requirements would be cause for celebration—or at least relief. "Never mind the *best*. Just let me know that our practices are *good enough* and I'll be happy."

The goal of this briefing is to move managers beyond anxiety and fear—and beyond "ADA minimalism"—into a new way of thinking that puts the ADA into its proper perspective and turns it into a management opportunity. The fundamental idea is to create an approach for meeting the ADA requirements that does not compromise sound human resource (HR) policy but enhances it, that does not thwart productivity but unleashes it, that does not burden managers but empowers them. This is what characterizes best practices under the ADA.

This idea may sound like a fantasy, or simply a bad case of wishful thinking. But this is precisely the attitude that has carried many successful firms into compliance with the basic principles of ADA, even before the statutes were written. As one manager from AT&T put it, "[The ADA] is an opportunity to reemphasize what we've been doing for years." For AT&T, and for many other firms, long-standing success in employing people with disabilities stems from understanding that such individuals are at least as safe, productive, and reliable as their non-disabled co-workers. In short, they consider employees with disabilities with very much the same attitudes as they do all other employees.

In terms of how managers approach the two groups (people with disabilities and those without), the similarities are, on the whole, greater than the differences. Managers seek to improve the performance of non-disabled employees; they bring the same concern to employees with disabilities. As managers provide tools, equipment, and training for non-disabled workers, so do they for employees with disabilities. As they recognize and respond to limitations and problems with non-disabled employees, so it is with employees with disabilities.

Some data may help demonstrate the point. Du Pont, long recognized as a leader in employing people with disabilities, conducts a periodic survey of its employees to determine, among other things, how those with disabilities compare with other workers on several important measures. The chart in Exhibit I.1 presents data for recent years. The results argue that employees with disabilities perform as well as others, have a comparable safety record, and attend work only slightly less frequently than the non-disabled employees.

In a similar vein, the cost of accommodating people with disabilities is much lower than might be expected. According to data collected by the Job Accommodation Network, the technical assistance arm of the President's Committee on Employment of People with Disabilities, the average cost of accommodation is less than $100 per person. The distribution of costs (see Exhibit I.2) suggests that many employees with disabilities can be hired with little or no financial investment for accommodations. Costs of this low magnitude are reasonable and manageable even for smaller companies. For larger firms, high-end accommodation costs for a few staff members will not significantly affect the total personnel budget.

Exhibit I.1. Overall performance comparison.

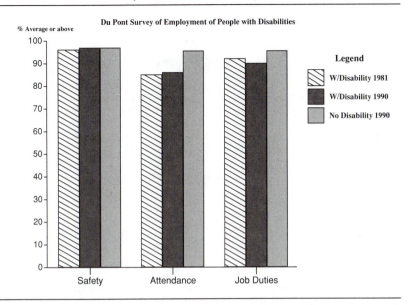

Du Pont Survey of Employment of People with Disabilities

% Average or above

Legend

W/Disability 1981

W/Disability 1990

No Disability 1990

Safety   Attendance   Job Duties

In this briefing, we will examine the ADA and its implications from many perspectives, including a few of the myths and stereotypes surrounding the ADA and the employment of people with disabilities. Our objective is to ensure that human resource and line managers can approach the ADA like good managers—informed and equipped with the best available knowledge and tools for implementation. The practices we will review and recommend focus on a *management* approach, i.e., one designed to meet the needs of managers. More will be said about this shortly.

BENCHMARKING EMPLOYMENT UNDER THE ADA

The term *benchmarking* has come into vogue with the popularity of total quality management (TQM). Its use has been largely in areas where quantification comes easily—manufacturing proc-

Exhibit I.2. Cost of job accommodations.

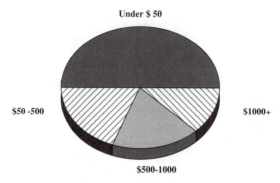

Under $ 50

$50 -500

$1000+

$500-1000

Source: Job Accommodation Network

ess control, inventory management, customer response analysis, and so forth. Human resource issues, like the ADA, may seem too "soft" for benchmarking. But through the efforts of companies like Xerox, managers are learning that the concepts of TQM, if not the specific methods, can be usefully applied to employment functions and processes.

Our use of the benchmarking concept consists of identifying the "best practices" of ADA implementation. The standards for ranking an approach as a best practice are twofold:

- The effectiveness and efficiency of a practice in making the ADA an integral part of a high-quality human resource management program; and
- Conformity with guidance from the federal government, particularly the Equal Employment Opportunity Commission, on what constitutes effective ADA compliance.

These criteria focus on the organization's need to function well at the same time that it meets the legal requirements of the ADA.

GOOD MANAGEMENT AS THE KEY PRINCIPLE

From the perspective of the first criterion (effectively integrating the ADA into a high-quality HR program), best practices center on the very essence of good management: guiding employees toward greater productivity, liberating them from the burdens of disorganization without saddling them with restrictive bureaucracy, and helping them to overcome some measure of the troublesome flaws inherent in people and processes. These are the measures of effectiveness and efficiency.

However, the problem with applying management principles and concepts such as these to the ADA comes not from the principles themselves, but from how managers see reality when legal issues obstruct the view. (Under these conditions—to paraphrase Mae West—"A good manager is hard to find.") The management guru, Peter Drucker, once said, "Much of what we call management consists of making it difficult for people to work." This is even more true on matters like ADA, where the "fear factor" runs high. The tendency is to retreat to a safe harbor of restrictive and narrow legal applications, or worse, to run for the cover of the legal department, abandoning the ship of management altogether. The effect of these approaches to the ADA can be demoralizing and counterproductive.

The most basic cause of fear comes when managers look primarily to the attorneys for guidance. While many attorneys have valuable knowledge about the ADA, they are usually not managers. The differences in approach are summarized in Exhibit I.3. The attorneys' orientation focuses, in general, on conformity to the details of the law and on litigation avoidance (or victory in court if litigation becomes unavoidable). This is not intrinsically bad. In fact, under some circumstances, this orientation can be quite useful. But a litigation-avoidance mentality blocks managers from approaching the issue as managers. Let the lawyers be lawyers; ask them to review what managers develop, not create management tools for them.

The personnel administrator shares the attorney's attention

Exhibit I.3. Different orientations toward legal issues.

GENERAL ORIENTATION

Legal details	Administrative details	Operational effectiveness	Organizational direction
Reduce risk	Reduce error	Maximize productivity	Maximize opportunity
LAWYER	**ADMINIS-TRATOR**	**MANAGER**	**LEADER**
Letter of the law	Forms and procedures	Management processes	Culture of non-discrimination
Potential problems	Micro-level emphasis	Macro-level emphasis	Potential opportunity

ADA ORIENTATION

to the details of the law—dot the "i" and cross the "t," fill out the right form, check to be sure the application asks only the right questions, and so on. Above all, the administrator wants to make sure to avoid any fatal process error. As with attorneys, personnel administrators need to have this orientation and attention to detail. No one would want it any other way. An effective ADA management program will include well-handled administrative detail, but only as a component of the total management picture, not its driving force.

The manager, while caring about the details, must keep in mind a host of larger concerns: performance, productivity, interpersonal dynamics, responsiveness to customers, costs, schedules, and long-term strategic planning. Managers cannot afford to focus too much attention for too long on the intricacies of every issue. This is the very problem that the ADA has created for many managers, inducing a paralysis of excessive worry about detail—a case of legal overload. When management of the ADA starts from the bottom up, i.e., when it begins with the legal and administrative details, managers cannot maintain the critical distances necessary for seeing the ADA in context within the whole picture of HR management.

The leadership role that managers are increasingly being encouraged to assume can become a means to a very positive end. As the diagram in Exhibit I.3 shows, the manager who becomes a leader takes the larger view and orients the team in the right direction. Stephen Covey addresses the issue well in his book, *Principle-Centered Leadership*. To Covey, what is needed in today's world is a "compass" that takes precedence over the "maps" we use for navigation. He says,

> I see several compelling reasons why the compass is so invaluable to corporate leaders:
>
> - The compass orients people to the coordinates and indicates a course or direction even in forests, deserts, seas, and open, unsettled terrain.
> - As the territory changes, the map becomes obsolete; in times of rapid change, a map may be dated and inaccurate by the time it's printed.
> - Inaccurate maps are sources of great frustration for people who are trying to find their way or navigate territory. . . .
> - The map provides description, but the compass provides more vision and direction.
> - An accurate map is a good management tool, but a compass is a leadership and empowerment tool.

The evolving implementation and application of the ADA puts us into the type of landscape that calls for a "compass": unsettled territory, changing terrain, inaccurate maps. The employees of an organization with any ADA responsibility need both the compass of the leader and the maps of the manager.

In light of this discussion, we can offer the first "best practice" in ADA implementation:

Practice # 1

Articulate clearly and disseminate widely the first principle of the ADA: nondiscrimination against people with disabilities.

Many business people opposed the ADA but agreed with its goal of eliminating discrimination. This goal is the ADA's "compass." The companies where the ADA is most effectively implemented begin with this first principle; then, from it, develop the "maps" for managers. That is why so many of the firms doing best with the ADA were already doing most of what the ADA requires—as they focused on the principle, the rest followed naturally. As we noted earlier, managers who start with the details of the maps are soon lost in the woods. The leadership role of top level management and HR managers on the ADA will be to ensure that everyone within the organization understands the first principle, even if some are slow to catch the details of the maps.

The dissemination of this principle plays an important part in the effective implementation of the ADA. A communications strategy is essential. The elements can include newsletters, posters, bulletin board announcements, or any other vehicle that will reach employees. It is important to remember the most basic tenet of effective communication: There is no communication unless the target audience actually receives the message correctly. Plan for some mechanism to determine whether the key managers and supervisors have understood the first principle of the ADA. Also, as we have all learned, memory fails. Reminders are essential.

One major element of both the message and the communications plan should be attitudinal awareness. No aspect of ADA implementation is more needed, or potentially more beneficial, than this one. For the ADA's first principle to take hold with employees at all levels within the organization, the organization must use training and other methods to communicate, effectively, the ways in which misperceptions and discriminatory attitudes lead to acts of discrimination. The thread of nondiscriminatory attitudes weaves throughout all ADA efforts, and in many respects, binds them all together.

INTEGRATION OF THE ADA INTO THE HR FUNCTION

In the beginning stages of its implementation, the ADA has come front and center—its provisions presented and discussed, debated and decried. Such visibility is unavoidable. But for the ADA to work well within the context of a high-quality human resource management program, it must ultimately become so routine that it blends into the walls.

The process by which this integration occurs takes time. The first stage, getting the first principle of nondiscrimination before the organization, requires both an initial effort and an ongoing reminder. The second stage of "map development," that is, using the regulations and creating or revising forms, policies, and procedures, requires focused staff effort and may take a good measure of time, depending, of course, on how well the company has done in setting the course prior to the ADA. The final stage involves the deployment of the ADA in all phases of the organization. Each of these activities must be given careful attention until a satisfactory comfort level has been reached.

But while the ADA effort takes time, HR managers should be moving the organization toward the goal and marking the ways in which the integration is taking place. When campus recruiters, for example, adopt a routine procedure for ensuring that recruiting sites are accessible, they will hardly have to think about it—they send the forms to the school with the normal packets of information and simply check to confirm that this one additional element has been addressed along with the others. The distraction is minimal because it has now been integrated into routine operations. The HR manager can see and note that one more step has been made toward integration of the first principle of nondiscrimination into the organizational routine.

This leads to the second of the ADA "best practices":

Practice # 2

Establish the ADA's first principle of nondiscrimination against people with disabilities as part of the organizational culture.

This practice obviously follows from the first one. The emphasis here, however, is for the long term. The goal of integration of the ADA into management routines calls for the same kinds of actions as have been used for race, sex, and age discrimination—simply creating an environment where nondiscrimination is understood as a given. Hewlett-Packard has been very effective in this respect. Each year, H-P holds a National Barrier Awareness Day to identify any barriers to employment of people with disabilities that may exist in any H-P operation around the country. The attitudinal component, as noted earlier, is central.

In at least one respect, the timing of the ADA could not be better, particularly for companies trying to implement diversity efforts. The meaning of *Workforce 2000* to employers was principally that diversity would increasingly be the norm; management styles and routines would need to reflect this reality. The ADA, in that respect, expands the thinking about diversity to include those employees or candidates with physical or mental disabilities. As organizations attempt to promote tolerance and to build on the inherent strengths of a diverse workforce, people with disabilities become part of the productive mix.

CONFORMITY WITH FEDERAL GOVERNMENT GUIDANCE

Recall our second criterion for benchmarking ADA practices: that they should conform with the guidance issued by the federal government, particularly EEOC. Regardless of the experiences managers may have had with federal agencies, on the ADA the government has been comparatively effective. In fact, much of what is being sold in the marketplace as tools for compliance either comes directly from the federal government or has an available counterpart in federally published materials. Although it may not have done so for other major legislative acts, the federal government has developed materials addressing some of the very practical issues managers face with ADA implementation.

Since enforcement comes through EEOC, the more good management can be advanced while keeping an eye on EEOC, the greater the likelihood of effective interpretation and application of the regulations. Despite what we have said thus far about starting from the first principle (the compass) and not from the details, as the maxim goes, "elegance is in the details." Bringing all the details into compliance puts form on the concept of nondiscrimination.

HOW TO READ THIS BOOK

What follows in this briefing are primarily maps for implementation, created for managers. The maps attempt to integrate "good management" with the principle of nondiscrimination on the basis of disability. They are not the only maps, but they represent some of the best thinking to this point.

As we proceed, it is important to remember the first best practice: do not focus on the maps so intensely that you lose sight of the compass. Without a clear sense of "true north," you will be like those who build the finest house in the world on the wrong lot, or who fight a great battle against the wrong enemy.

1

Job Descriptions

One of the ADA issues of seemingly greatest concern to managers, at least in these early days of implementation, centers on job or position descriptions. This may be due, at least in part, to the near panic that sometimes sweeps over managers when they realize how outdated many of their job descriptions [probably] are. That feeling, coupled with a back-of-an-envelope estimate of the time involved in trying to bring them up to date, can point toward a task of monstrous proportions.

This fear of job descriptions under the ADA has enough basis in reality to make it a legitimate issue, but not enough to cause the level of worry that seems to pervade seminars and meetings when the subject arises. The ADA does not *require* companies to have job descriptions, and EEOC has stated this position clearly:

> The ADA does not require an employer to develop or maintain job descriptions. A written job description that is prepared before advertising or interviewing applicants for a job will be considered as evidence along with other relevant factors. However, the job description will not be given greater weight than other relevant evidence.

The proper perspective on job descriptions, then, considers them important but not uniquely or absolutely so. While job descriptions are likely to become one significant part of the picture, we do not want to place an inordinate weight upon them, to the detriment of other aspects of implementation, or even more importantly, to the detriment of the organization's effectiveness.

With that caveat in mind, let's recognize that current and accurate job descriptions can be quite useful under the ADA, providing legal support as well as a management tool for HR staff and line managers. The key is to invest sufficient time and effort to do what needs to be done, but to do so without initiating a massive project for which managers do *not* have time. The best practices in this area create the *mechanism* for revising job descriptions without upsetting the HR apple cart:

Practice # 3

Prepare or revise job descriptions as an ongoing, not a one-time, activity.

This practice follows EEOC's guidance. Recall that the EEOC associates the revision or development of job descriptions with "advertising or interviewing applicants for a job."

The implications are quite clear: The revision of job descriptions need not be done as a major one-time effort, particularly any time soon, but rather as one step in a routine HR function. Except in the unlikely situation that HR staff have substantial amounts of free time, there is nothing to warrant a comprehensive job description overhaul. In fact, doing so may be counterproductive.

An example may help to illustrate this point. One firm, and a generally good firm by almost every measure, decided to look at every job or position description within the organization to determine whether these accurately reflected the current tasks and requirements of individuals in the position. The company's approach took the following steps:

- A task force of HR staff was created to analyze all job descriptions;
- The task force went on site at the various company locations to gather information on all positions;
- For each position or job, the task force performed a detailed time/motion/effort/requirements analysis; and
- Created revised position descriptions.

On the surface, this company's efforts sound fine, even admirable for their diligence and thoroughness. There is, however, one major concern about a comprehensive effort like this. If the approach to the process contains a weakness or flaw, that basic error will be replicated in every description. Consequently, the staff may have to mount a second (duplicate) effort to correct the errors of the first round. And that was precisely what happened in this case.

What, specifically, was wrong with this firm's approach? Several things:

- The effort was not necessary at that time; the firm was not hiring any new employees and none of the current employees had a disability requiring an accommodation. As a result, a substantial amount of key staff time was arguably wasted. (The mitigating factor in this example was that the firm was not doing any hiring at all, leaving employment managers with time on their hands. Thus, the activity helped prevent a layoff of HR staff.)
- The approach assumed that the way the job was currently conducted was the method the job *required*. In other words, without a compelling need to do so, the company cast each task in concrete. Quite likely, the firm will need to crack the concrete each time a creative employee or supervisor redesigns the task or a new piece of equipment is added.
- In one specific instance, employees were required to move from job to job within a flexible staffing system. The problem here, relative to the ADA, lay in the fact that the

task force unilaterally assumed that every employee had to be qualified to do every assignment that people in that position category were ever called upon to do. This unnecessarily increased the minimum physical requirements for every employee. By making all the tasks "essential" for everyone, the company virtually eliminated the flexibility to accommodate an individual with the ability to do *most* tasks.

One example from the appendix to the ADA employment regulations may help to illustrate the problem:

• Suppose a Sack Handler position requires that the employee pick up fifty pound sacks and carry them from the company loading dock to the storage room, and that a sack handler who is disabled by a back impairment requests a reasonable accommodation. Upon receiving the request, the employer analyzes the Sack Handler job and determines that the essential function and purpose of the job is not the requirement that the job holder physically lift and carry the sacks, but the requirement that the job holder cause the sack to move from the loading dock to the storage room.

As this example shows, the issue for identifying "essential functions" in a job description is not *how* you want the job accomplished, but *what* you want the employee to accomplish.

The company in question had a number of warehouse positions very much like the sack handler. By "calibrating" these jobs in terms of lifting requirements (pounds) and carrying requirements (feet of distance), the task force created the almost certain possibility that the descriptions would be short lived. If any one of these requirements changes before the next position opening, they will need to re-do the specifications. It is quite easy to imagine that suppliers could change box sizes, or that tables or other loading surfaces could be rearranged to alter the carrying distance, or that a new piece of equipment such as a conveyor, small forklift, or dolly could be put into use. Any of these changes would affect the job requirements and require an alteration in what had become identified as the "essential functions."

This example points to the kinds of management problems that can arise with the ADA: In their enthusiasm to comply, an HR staff may waste resources, restrict opportunities for people with disabilities, and effectively box in their own line managers. The better way, as our "best practice" suggests, is to review or create the job description at the time of a related HR activity, such as a vacancy announcement or performance review, incorporating the best assessment of the essential functions at the time.

HOW TO CREATE AN ADA-COMPLIANT JOB DESCRIPTION

Our discussion of the management issues related to overly narrow specifications of essential job functions demonstrates the problems to avoid in this arena. This leads naturally to our next benchmark practice for the development of ADA-compliant job descriptions. But before we present this practice, a brief aside.

One new category of products on the market includes software packages that claim to "guarantee" your success in writing ADA-compliant job descriptions. These products must be recognized for what they are: tools that may (or may not) save you time or effort, but that surely cannot guarantee ADA compliance. The idea behind the guarantee is that the *form* of the job description—the kinds of words that are used, the sequence of the key words, and the way the words are laid out on a page—matters most. Following this logic will *not* ensure that what you have written will comply with the ADA. At best, the exercise will help you to think of useful descriptive words and put the descriptors into a form that is clearer and easier to understand. For many HR managers, that may serve a very useful purpose, but it must not be thought of as de facto satisfaction of ADA requirements. This is true for several reasons, not the least of which is that (as noted earlier) the ADA has no job description requirements!

What is legitimately meant, then, by trying to create ADA-compliant job descriptions? The first and foremost consideration comes from this "best practice":

Practice # 4

Focus job descriptions on the essential functions or tasks, not the method for doing them.

This basic principle lies at the heart of the ADA's approach to employment. If managers understand this, they will not only see how the job description comes into play under the ADA, but how the entire employment process was designed to work when hiring people with disabilities.

First, by focusing on functions or tasks rather than methods for doing the tasks, we gain insight into a critical distinction under the ADA. As the EEOC technical assistance manual points out, "A job analysis will be most helpful for purposes of the ADA if it focuses on the **results** or **outcome** of a function, not solely on the way it is customarily performed."

The manual continues with these examples:

- An essential function of a computer programmer job might be described as "ability to develop programs that accomplish necessary objectives," rather than "ability to manually write programs." Although a person currently performing the job may write these programs by hand, that is not the essential function, because programs can be developed directly on the computer.
- If a job requires mastery of information contained in technical manuals, this essential function would be "ability to learn technical material," rather than "ability to read technical manuals." People with visual and other reading impairments could perform this function using other means, such as audiotapes.

- A job that requires objects to be moved from one place to another should state this essential function. The analysis may note that the person in this job needs to "lift 50 pound cartons to a height of 3 or 4 feet and load them into truck-trailers 5 hours daily," but should not identify the "ability to *manually* lift and load 50 pound cartons" as an essential function unless this is the only method by which the function can be performed without causing an undue hardship.

This last example clearly relates to our previous discussion about the sack handler and helps to expand the concept of essential functions. It is perfectly appropriate to define the lift-and-carry requirements if there is no other alternative. The management challenge and opportunity is to determine whether this is the only way.

A COMPASS READING FOR ESSENTIAL FUNCTIONS

The distinction we have made between tasks and methods may seem like the ultimate in legal nitpicking. We need to get back to our "true north" perspective and view the quality-of-management issues (best practices) from that vantage point, rather than through the lawyer's eyes. As a way back, consider the second EEOC example just given regarding the mastery of technical materials. In the example, EEOC said that the essential function would be the "ability to learn technical material" rather than the "ability to read technical manuals." Why worry about the distinction?

First, from the ADA "true north" point of view, the goal is nondiscrimination on the basis of disability. In other words, organizations need to eliminate any barrier that would prevent a qualified individual with a disability from enjoying all the benefits and privileges of employment. Barriers can take many forms, and even a single word or phrase has the potential to mean the difference between unemployment and a job. The language of "reading" (vs. "learning") subtly communicates a limited view of what individuals can accomplish. If everyone involved with the hiring decision could readily do the translation, the language would probably not constitute a real barrier, but that is often not the case.

Line managers or supervisors, unless they have been trained in disability awareness or have learned from their own experience, may well struggle to envision how a person who cannot read technical manuals could still learn the material. If the manuals are not available in alternative formats (Braille, audiotape, large print), the problem seems rather obvious. Only when a management decision is made to provide the materials in an alternative format or through another accommodation (a reader or a scanning computer with audio readout capability) can the individual with the disability be legitimately considered "qualified" for the job. At this point, the subtle technicality becomes a very real barrier to an otherwise qualified candidate.

As with race, ethnicity, sex, religion, national origin or any other category of protected class of individuals under civil rights laws, subtlety in language can make a major difference. Without a clear informed vision of the principle of nondiscrimination, the subtleties are lost on all but the one who experiences discrimination as a result. The best companies in employment of people with disabilities have created a sensitivity to nuance in language and expectation that recognizes when a very small point has very large ramifications.

From the larger perspective of effective management, the distinction between "reading manuals" and "learning materials" has several possible implications:

- The entire organization or division could decide to move completely away from using technical manuals to interactive video training or on-line help systems, all or some of which could have audio readout capability or graphic icons in lieu of words;
- A technical troubleshooting function could be organized into a work team where one individual takes on the major

responsibility for reading the manuals while another does the hands-on work, thereby eliminating the need for some members of the team to read the manuals at all;

- With the rather troubling problem of illiteracy, as well as the increasing number of non-English speaking employees, the company may choose to accept individuals with high technical skills but limited reading capabilities. These firms must either live with the challenges or, as some have done, teach the new employees to read English.

It is not hard to imagine any of these scenarios. The consequence of any one of them would be to make the second option for describing essential functions ("learning technical material") more desirable and more appropriate than the first.

Determining Essential Functions

The discussions of essential functions, thus far, have not formally identified the criteria for determining what really is essential, according to the ADA itself and the EEOC regulations and technical guidance. A job function can be considered essential if it meets one or more of the following criteria:

- *The position exists to perform the function*—A word processing operator must be able to do word processing at the company's required level of speed and accuracy; a night supervisor must be available to work at night; a truck driver must have the appropriate license to drive a truck.
- *There are a limited number of other employees available to perform the function, or among whom the function can be distributed*— For example, night clerks in a convenience store typically must do many different tasks because there is no one else available to do them; or, having a very small maintenance staff may necessitate that each staff member be able to do a wide variety of tasks.
- *A function is highly specialized, and the person in the position is*

hired for special expertise or ability to perform it—Most duties of a medical technician, doctor, or nurse require a person with that expertise; if, in the case of a computer hardware specialist, the individual's expertise was necessary to sort through library materials properly, visits to the library might be considered part of an essential function.

The EEOC regulations and technical assistance materials also identify several other types of "evidence" that a job function is essential:

• *The employer's judgment*—An employer can set proper performance standards and hold employees to them, but employers should be sure that the standards are justified and are actually maintained within the organization. As we have discussed, the judgment should also take into account the possibility of alternative means.

• *A written job description prepared before advertising or interviewing applicants for a job*—This is a bit circular, but it recognizes that properly prepared job descriptions help to define the essential functions.

• *The amount of time spent performing the function*—While there are no absolute standards for this determination, a function that occupies a major portion of the person's time is clearly included as essential; activities on the low end of the time graph probably need to be justified on other grounds.

• *The consequences of not requiring a person in this job to perform a function*—It is essential for a fireman to be able to carry a person from a burning building and for a pilot to land a plane; in either case, the consequences of failure could be very serious. However, if a clerical worker is asked to cover phones occasionally and cannot do so because of a disability, failure to catch all the calls would not be a serious problem. (It could also, of course, be handled with an answering machine.)

• *The terms of a collective bargaining agreement*—These agreements often identify what an individual should or should not do within a specific job classification. While not absolute, they can be considered as part of the overall determination of essential functions.

• *Work experience of people who have performed a job in the past and work experience of people who currently perform similar jobs*—The experience of these individuals provides real-world evidence of what a job actually requires. As discussed earlier in the job analysis process, this grounding in what actually goes on is one of the clear management considerations under the ADA.

• *Other relevant factors*—Ah yes, the "other" category. Two kinds of considerations are specifically mentioned by EEOC under this topic: the *nature of the work operation*, as for example, under a flexible manufacturing system or "just-in-time" inventory operation; or the employer's *organizational structure*, including use of work teams in which tasks are rotated among individuals on the team.

Analyzing every job function under all these considerations can be a daunting task. Many companies and organizations have developed checklists to try to simplify the process. The one presented in Exhibit 1.1 can be used or modified for this purpose. The value of this particular checklist is its simplicity; the amount of time spent filling out forms is kept to a minimum by the "circle-the-number" approach. For a more detailed analysis, a form like the one in Exhibit 1.2 may be used. Larger firms have created forms such as this one for use by their HR staff. Smaller firms may find the simpler form to be more effective.

THE JOB ANALYSIS PROCESS

The development of a job description almost always calls for an analysis of the job requirements. While the ADA does not mandate a job analysis any more than it requires job descriptions, an effective management approach will invariably include this step to the extent possible. The best approach to the job analysis process involves one key element:

Practice # 5

Make job analysis an interactive process engaging managers, supervisors, and staff in dialogue to identify essential job functions.

While this approach can become very time-consuming, the involvement of all the key players is the only way to determine effectively and accurately how the job is currently being done and precisely what functions can be properly considered essential. The critical factor for an effective job analysis, according to the EEOC, is that it "focus on the purpose of the job and the importance of actual job functions in achieving this purpose." This follows much of our previous discussion about "tasks" vs. "methods" for doing the job. The central theme: Remain open to the possibility of another way to do it.

The steps in an effective job analysis should ideally include:

- Reviewing any documentation available, including current job or position descriptions, as well as any management reports on the operations of the unit or division;
- Interviewing line managers and supervisors for their assessment of the position requirements and essential functions;
- Interviewing current employees in the job or position, if possible, to learn from them about the actual job requirements (*results*) and what issues they see for effective performance of the job;
- Conducting an on-site observation to see firsthand what the job involves and to identify issues that need to be resolved, such as differences in the opinions of managers, supervisors, and employees about the job requirements, or changes in work steps that might be instituted to improve efficiency;

Exhibit 1.1. Essential functions analysis No. 1.

Categories

0. No reason to consider essential.
1. Employees in this position are actually required to do this function.
2. The position exists to perform the particular function.
3. There are too few people available to do this function.
4. Special expertise is required to do this function.
5. A high percentage of time is spent performing this function.

Note: More than one reason may be needed to establish the function as "essential."

FUNCTION	REASON FOR CONSIDERING ESSENTIAL					
_____	0	1	2	3	4	5
_____	0	1	2	3	4	5
_____	0	1	2	3	4	5
_____	0	1	2	3	4	5
_____	0	1	2	3	4	5
_____	0	1	2	3	4	5
_____	0	1	2	3	4	5
_____	0	1	2	3	4	5
_____	0	1	2	3	4	5
_____	0	1	2	3	4	5
_____	0	1	2	3	4	5

- Revising or creating the job or position description based upon the input and observations;
- Checking back with the managers, supervisors, and staff to see whether the new description captures all the essential functions; and
- Making any needed changes and finalizing the description.

A process like this will provide the information needed to differentiate essential from nonessential functions under the ADA.

HR managers may find that this job-analysis process provides a good opportunity to educate management and staff about the ADA, the notion of "essential functions," and the concept of reasonable accommodation (to be discussed later in this briefing). It will be important, during the job analysis, to give HR staff enough perspective to be helpful in possible methods changes.

FLEXIBLE MANAGEMENT AND ADA JOB DESCRIPTIONS

Peter Drucker, Tom Peters, Ken Blanchard, and virtually every other management analyst has rightly pointed to the need for management flexibility in today's rapidly changing business environment. Consider, for example, the ways in which science and technology have changed the requirements and qualifications for employees in nearly every job category over the past decade. Auto mechanics now deal more with computers than carburetors; accountants seldom need calculators now that electronic database programs do all the numerical manipulation; grocery checkout clerks spend most of their time sliding products across a glass screen. With such rapid and substantial change, management must be able to change job structures, methods, tools and equipment, skill requirements, and so forth. The flexibility to make these changes should not be inhibited by a misapplication of one component of the ADA.

Exhibit 1.2. Essential functions analysis No. 2.

FUNCTION	POSITION EXISTS TO PERFORM	CURRENTLY REQUIRED	ESTIMATED % TIME TOTAL = 100%	NO. OF PEOPLE AVAILABLE TO PERFORM	IMPACT IF NOT DONE BY THIS PERSON	LEVEL OF SPECIALIZED EXPERTISE REQUIRED	RESULTS OF ANALYSIS	COMMENTS
	— Yes — No If yes, function is essential	— Yes — No	—— %	——	— Serious problem — Incon-venience — Not a problem	— High — Moderate — Low	— Essential — Marginal — Non-essential	
	— Yes — No If yes, function is essential	— Yes — No	—— %	——	— Serious problem — Incon-venience — Not a problem	— High — Moderate — Low	— Essential — Marginal — Non-essential	
	— Yes — No If yes, function is essential	— Yes — No	—— %	——	— Serious problem — Incon-venience — Not a problem	— High — Moderate — Low	— Essential — Marginal — Non-essential	
	— Yes — No If yes, function is essential	— Yes — No	—— %	——	— Serious problem — Incon-venience — Not a problem	— High — Moderate — Low	— Essential — Marginal — Non-essential	

These kinds of changes have been the major cause of the grim reality that all too many job descriptions on file do not reflect current tasks or requirements. One great benefit of integrating job analysis/job description writing into the announcement and performance evaluation efforts comes from the flexibility it gives managers to change these documents to reflect current reality. This flexibility is critical.

The best practices under the ADA do not interfere with management flexibility, but build on it. The job description process must be as fluid as the organization's operations, able to be changed to meet changing demands, structured to follow rather than lead the work of effective management. Job descriptions cannot become monoliths, stone objects that resist modification and stall the company's movement.

JOB DESCRIPTIONS WITHIN WORK TEAMS

The use of work teams or project teams raises special issues, specifically when the team's tasks cannot be clearly divided among the team members. The team approach has gained prominence among managers as a method for creating the synergy a company needs to increase productivity, quality, and speed in developing products. This very useful management approach introduces new challenges and opportunities—for management in general and for the ADA in particular.

Consider one example. A team has the responsibility to develop a new software package. Each member must contribute to the effort. Some may bring hardware expertise, others software expertise, others knowledge of the marketplace. Together they create the product, with each team member being part of the process. The job descriptions would, in this case, focus on the "essential functions" of both the individual team member, as well as the tasks before the team. For the hardware expert, the essential functions might include the following:

• Research the state of the art in personal computer hardware applications related to the ABC software development project;

- Report to the team on relevant hardware issues; and
- Participate in team meetings.

These essential functions do not specify requirements that could be discriminatory against a person with a disability, nor do they limit the necessary interaction of team members in accomplishing the objectives of creating new software.

However, if the job description were changed to what some have envisioned as an ADA-compliant description, the functions might look something like this:

- Read documents in the corporate library and search on-line databases to gather information on the state of the art in personal computer hardware applications related to the ABC software development project;
- Provide written and oral reports on the research to the project team; and
- Participate in team meetings.

What is wrong with these descriptions? They are too specific about the methods for doing the tasks. The first function requires the individual to use resources that may not be accessible to him or her: a wheelchair user may find the corporate library inaccessible, or an individual with vision impairments may not be able to access on-line databases unless the system were equipped with voice simulation capabilities. The person hired probably does not need to read the documents *in* the library. Unless there are security measures that prohibit document removal, another team member or an administrative staff person could retrieve the material. Similarly, for a person with a severe speech impairment, oral reports would be impossible. But he or she could likely provide the same information as effectively through a written, graphic, or computer image-based presentation.

The goal of not unnecessarily restricting the essential functions as they appear in the job descriptions applies not only under the ADA but to any good team management system. The keys to effective work teams, particularly within a quality management system, focus on the ability of team members to relate well with each other, to be creative, and to contribute to constant improvements in methods and systems for accomplishing the work objectives. As a step toward this kind of a quality system, management experts are encouraging the development of broader job descriptions and responsibilities. The characteristics of a good team member are not well defined by conventional task descriptors.

SAMPLE JOB DESCRIPTIONS

The following job descriptions, provided by the President's Committee on Employment of People with Disabilities, clarify and reinforce the best practices articulated in this chapter.

POSITION TITLE: Manager, Personnel Financial Services
DEPARTMENT: General Accounting and Administration
Financial Services
REPORTS TO: Manager, Administrative Financial Services

DESCRIBE THE BROAD FUNCTION AND SCOPE OF THE POSITION:

This person is responsible for providing direct support and services to the company personnel department on financial issues; accounting for and providing financial/budgeting consultation to health care and dental care operations; fringe accounting; providing direct support and services to the company aviation department on financial issues; assists in analysis of GAE actual to budget for accountability reporting; assists in accounting for additional reserves from corporate pushdown; balance sheet account analysis; various governmental reports; and special projects as requested. The incumbent in this position works closely with the company senior vice president of personnel and his direct reports on financial and budgeting issues relating to personnel.

DESCRIBE THE PRINCIPAL CONTINUING ACCOUNTABILITIES OF THE POSITION IN ORDER OF IMPORTANCE:

1. Provide direct support and service to the personnel department on all accounting, budgeting, and financial issues relative to personnel, the health care and dental care operations, and employee benefits.
2. Provide direct support and services to the aviation department on all accounting, budgeting, and financial issues.
3. Provide guidance and assistance for general ledger and financial reporting functions for health care and dental care operations.
4. Forecast, account for, and report fringe expenses for all payroll.
5. Develop and maintain the balance sheet account analysis procedures.
6. Provide assistance in GAE analysis of actual to budget for accountability reporting.
7. Provide assistance as requested for special projects.

POSITION TITLE: Credit Application
                                   Solicitor—Retail
JOB CODE: 3040
REPRESENTATIVE DUTIES:

- Solicits new credit accounts on the selling floor.
- Provides an opening line presentation to the customer.
- Explains the benefits of opening an account to the customer.
- Asks the customer to fill out a credit application.
- Reviews the application to be sure that it is filled out correctly.
- Qualifies each customer to find out if he or she is of credit age.
- Uses gifts and premiums to encourage the customer to complete an application.

JOB TITLE: Assembler/Packer
DIVISION/DEPARTMENT: Operations/Rectangle Dedicated
                                  Line
PURPOSE: (Include *primary accomplishments*, *products*, and *services*, *who* benefits from them and *how*.)

The purpose of the assembler/packer on the rectangle dedicated line is to complete a partially completed work surface and package it to standards.

ESSENTIAL JOB DUTIES: (What do you have to be able to do to achieve the desired results of your job? Include management and leadership responsibilities for work team leaders.)

- Visually inspects and transfers work surfaces into boring machine.
- Assembles and attaches understructures to work surface.

- Packages completed work surfaces, instruction sheets, and correct parts.
- Knows and adheres to standards of quality.

GENERAL DESCRIPTION: (How would you describe this job to someone who has never done it?)

This job has five workstations. One station has two people working together. Assemblers rotate between stations every two to four hours. Assemblers are responsible for making sure their co-workers know the correct parts that go with each work surface. Many assemblers perform tasks such as keeping the work area clean, maintaining the tape dispenser machine, gathering parts needed for assembly, sliding spacers on screws, etc.

They can refer to the booklet prepared by the quality control engineers (located at the line site) to learn quality standards.

The job is done while standing and working on a work surface that is 33 inches off the floor. The tools used are a Stratovac (pneumatic lifter), air driven, in-line screwdriver, and, infrequently, pliers. The product moves through the line at a rate of one every 1½ to 3 minutes. Work surfaces vary in size from 24″ × 24″ up to 30″ × 96″, and in weight from 27 to 116 pounds. They are lifted with a partner off the line, into a box, and onto a pallet. The highest point it is lifted is roughly six feet.

MINIMUM REQUIREMENTS: (What is required to perform the Essential Duties?)

- A minimum of three years of production experience.
- Ability to do essential duties.
- Ability to understand and follow English instructions.
- Ability to transfer 27–116 pounds a distance of six feet with help of another person.

2

Employee Selection

The ADA's employment provisions were designed to eliminate all barriers to employment of people with disabilities. Consequently, the Act's provisions cover all stages in the employment process, from the first elements of pre-employment to all post-employment activities.

This chapter looks at the pre-employment phase—from the first announcement of employment opportunities to the hiring decision—to identify the best practices for eliminating discrimination in these steps. Again, the key is to keep focused on "true north": the basic principle of nondiscrimination on the basis of disability.

Discrimination can take many forms in this phase. The goal is to eliminate them all. Although the sequence of pre-employment activities may change from company to company and job to job, most—if not all—of the activities discussed in this chapter fall within the realm of a typical pre-employment process. We will look at each one individually to identify the benchmarks for ADA compliance.

BARRIER-FREE RECRUITING

The ADA's goal of eliminating all barriers begins with recruiting. The ideal of "barrier-free recruiting" means that regardless of how an organization seeks candidates (by posted announcements, newspaper advertisements, campus recruiting, job fairs, executive search firms, or any other method), a qualified candidate with a disability will have equal opportunity to learn about and apply for a position. The benchmark practice can be stated this way:

Practice #6

> Ensure that recruiting practices provide qualified individuals with disabilities equal opportunity to become employment candidates.

This standard implies that any factor leading to an uneven playing field should be eliminated.

From the standpoint of effective management, the logic behind this practice relates to the ever-growing need to ensure that the organization locates and hires the best qualified candidates, disabled or not. Some of the most brilliant minds on earth belong to people whose disabilities would literally prevent them from getting in the door at some companies. Before Stephen Hawking, the world-renowned physicist and author of *A Brief History of Time*, achieved his current status, most recruiters would not have given this brilliant man a second look. Even now, some would see only his formidable disability and not his formidable ability.

Of course, not all people with disabilities (or anyone else for that matter) are like Stephen Hawking—and, thankfully, not all jobs require that level of mental ability. But consider the potential loss caused by discriminatory recruiting. Most of us have learned that good business practice means being careful not to prejudge candidates by their appearance alone. We want to keep that same good business sense when considering a candidate whose disability is more obvious than his or her ability.

One point needs to be made here. Typically, human resource staff are *not* the ones who create the problems of discrimination in employment. Rather, HR staff generally lead the way, using information and training to counter potentially prejudicial actions by line managers or supervisors. For many HR professionals, the ADA has become a catalyst for doing what they have tried to do for years—train managers in the ADA's first principle of nondiscrimination.

It may also be useful at this point to step back to ensure that the ADA's definition of a *person with a disability* is clear. Exhibit 2.1 presents the definition. Note that the ADA covers not only people who currently have a disability, but two other categories of individuals as well.

First, the ADA also protects people who are "regarded as having an impairment," even if they do not actually have one. Individuals in this group can be people who may act in unusual ways that lead an employer to believe they have a disability. It also includes those who have a cosmetic disfigurement that makes them look as though they have a disability. The protection provided by the ADA for these individuals is designed to ensure that a "decision of the first glance" does not prevent a qualified individual from pursuing employment. From a management perspective, we know that first impressions count for a lot. Thus, the provision implies that an individual should be given a second look to determine if his or her qualifications meet the standards for the position. Looking "beyond the first glance" may reveal a real gem of an employee.

Second, the ADA's protections extend to individuals who have a "record of an impairment." This category includes people with a history of substance abuse, previous claimants under workers' compensation, and individuals who have recovered from a debilitating physical condition. The objective is to prevent the employer from making a false assumption about the impact of the individual's history on his or her ability to work. Nothing in the pre-employment phase should bring this

Exhibit 2.1. Definition of disability.

A physical or mental impairment that substantially limits one or more major life activities; a record of such an impairment; or being regarded as having such an impairment.

Physical or Mental Impairment		Major Life Activities	Record of Impairment	Regarded as Impaired
Physiological disorder, contagious disease, cosmetic disfigurement or anatomical loss in one or more systems:	Mental or psychological disorder including:	Major life activities include:	The individual has:	The individual has:
• Neurological • Musculoskeletal • Respiratory • Cardiovascular • Reproductive • Digestive • Genito-urinary • Hemic • Lymphatic • Skin • Endocrine	• Mental retardation • Organic brain syndrome • Emotional or mental illness • Specific learning disabilities	• Self-care • Manual tasks • Walking • Seeing • Hearing • Speaking • Breathing • Learning • Working	• A history of impairment or • A record of having been misclassified as having an impairment	• An impairment not limiting major life activity, but treated as limiting by the firm; • An impairment limiting major life activity only as a result of attitudes or • No impairment, but treated by the firm as having one.
• Substance abuse				

information to the surface. If it does come up, it should not have a bearing on recruiting efforts or the hiring decision.

Job Advertisements and Notices

This is the first place to look for barriers to opportunity. For newspaper ads, if a phone number is included, a TDD number (see Exhibit 2.2), while not necessarily required by the ADA, should also be included, unless the state's relay service is operational. (If staff are taking calls related to the announcement, they should have a very short training session, or perhaps a simple memo, describing how to take a relay call.) Other general guidelines include:

- Post job announcements in an accessible location. Have the person responsible check to ensure that wheelchair users could enter the room, reach the board where the announcement is posted, and read it from chair height.
- As an alternative, place copies of the announcement on a table in an accessible location with a clearly marked sign, or make a staff person available to provide assistance.
- Provide voice recordings (e.g., "job lines") for people with vision impairments.

Also, potential applicants should be notified that the organization will provide reasonable accommodations.

Accessibility, On-Site and Off

Standards of nondiscrimination apply to all recruiting sites and the firm's employment or personnel offices as well as other locations, such as a college campus or conference center. The first consideration should be that these sites are physically accessible to people with disabilities, to the extent possible. In some cases, the cost of making facilities accessible might appear excessive, creating what the ADA calls an "undue hardship." But it is important not to reach the "undue hardship" conclusion too quickly. There are many ways to make a facility

Exhibit 2.2. What is a TDD?

A TDD, or telecommunications device for the deaf, is a piece of equipment that enables people with hearing or speech impairments to communicate by telephone. It resembles a typewriter and has three main parts: a QWERTY keyboard, a read-out display similar to a calculator (but with words rather than numbers), and a coupler that holds a telephone receiver.

Is it hard to use?

Not at all. It is as easy to use as a typewriter. The user simply types messages on the keyboard and sees the messages sent, as well as those received, on the read-out screen. TDD users have a few basic codes to simplify communications, such as ending each turn talking with the letters "GA" (meaning "go ahead") and shorthand forms of words, such as "pls" for "please." Even children can use a TDD, and training adults takes a matter of minutes. Most new TDDs come with instructions, including the communication codes.

Are special electrical connections needed?

No. All that is needed is a standard electrical outlet and a regular telephone.

Is it expensive?

Basic TDDs cost less than $200. With a built-in printer, the cost goes up by $100 to $200. More sophisticated TDDs can be purchased at higher costs, but most organizations need only the basic device.

Where do you buy them?

For the supplier in your area, contact a local organization for the deaf, a service agency for people with disabilities, or a disabled students office at a local college or university. Telecommunications for The Deaf, Inc., can also provide information; contact this organization at (301) 589-3006 (voice or TDD).

accessible, and some of the alternatives are really quite inexpensive. The principle or best practice to follow can be stated in this way:

Practice #7

Make it a rule to use only physically accessible recruiting sites and to provide materials in alternative formats.

Recruiters should make this a routine part of their off-site activities, and the firm should ensure that the employment office and any other sites where candidates come to get information are also accessible, as noted earlier. If the primary site is not accessible, use an equivalent site that is.

Most recruiters are experts in recruiting, not in inspecting site accessibility. Is it appropriate to expect them to evaluate a site? Yes. With a modest amount of training and a layman's checklist, recruiters can at least ensure that the major accessibility features are in place. The checklist in Exhibit 2.3 is one example of this kind of tool. As a point of information, most, if not all, sites for recruiting events (hotel meeting rooms, convention centers, college campuses) are covered by the ADA's public accommodations provisions, even though the institutions may not be aware of that fact.

Alternative Formats for Materials

Besides making recruiting sites accessible, the recruiting staff should prepare alternative formats for materials to be given to potential employment candidates. Written materials may be a problem for a visually impaired or blind applicant, and spoken information, similarly, may create a barrier for a person who is hard of hearing or deaf.

Low-cost accommodations in this area include:

- Preparing a large-print version of information on the company or position. A word processing program with large-font capabilities works very well for this.

(*Text continues on p. 48*)

Exhibit 2.3. Accessibility checklist.

Note: If you know who the attendees will be, you should contact them in advance to identify needed accessibility features and then ensure that these will be available. Some accommodations listed below may not be necessary; other accommodations not listed may be needed. Use creativity, courtesy, and common sense.

PARKING:

Yes   No

☐   ☐   Enough properly marked accessible spaces (sign with the universal access symbol), near an accessible entrance

☐   ☐   Each one 8' wide or wider, plus a 5' adjoining aisle

OUTDOOR ROUTE:

☐   ☐   Sidewalks 36" wide or wider for the full path leading to the main entrance

☐   ☐   Curb cuts where needed (36" wide or wider, with a smooth, gradual slope)

☐   ☐   Clear of obstructions, rough surfaces, snow/ice/leaves

ENTRANCE:

☐   ☐   Ramps with gradual slope (1:12), handrails, edge protection, non-slip surface

☐   ☐   Signs at non-accessible entrances pointing to an accessible entrance

☐   ☐   32" wide, easy opening hinge-type door or automatic doors

☐   ☐   Adequate maneuvering clearance (48" or more between doors in series)

☐   ☐   Thresholds ½" high or less or beveled

INTERIOR ROUTE:

☐   ☐   36" wide or more at all points with adequate turning room at corners

Yes   No

☐   ☐   Adequate clear floor space around protruding objects (furniture, plants, etc.)
☐   ☐   Non-slip surface
☐   ☐   No level changes over ½" without ramp
☐   ☐   Passenger (not freight) elevator, if needed, with adequate floor space, tactile call buttons at about 42" height, visible/audible signals, raised floor indicators

PUBLIC RESTROOMS:

☐   ☐   At least one wide stall for each gender with sturdy grab bars at 33–36" height, seat height of 17–19", non-obstructive door
☐   ☐   At least one accessible lavatory (34" or less to top surface, 29" or more knee clearance, clear floor space, under-counter pipes insulated, lever or electronic faucets)

MEETING ROOMS:

☐   ☐   On an accessible route (from the parking lot/outside entrance to the room)
☐   ☐   Entrance doors at least 32" wide with clear access to them, easy to open
☐   ☐   Clear floor space throughout for wheelchairs to maneuver
☐   ☐   Materials and refreshment tables clearly accessible and reachable
☐   ☐   Seating areas for wheelchairs distributed throughout the room
☐   ☐   Stage or platform large enough for wheelchairs to maneuver and properly ramped (gradual slope with handrails, edge protection, non-slip surface, 5' landing areas)
☐   ☐   Stairs have sturdy handrails on both sides
☐   ☐   Assistive listening device provided (permanent or portable)

- Making an audiotape recording of the same information. There is no need to use expensive equipment or professional recording services, as long as the tape and voice quality are sufficient to give a clear sound.
- Investigating the possibility of making Braille copies of basic company information. The ADA does not require this, and demand for this format may not be high. But if the firm has Braille materials available, it speaks well of the company's commitment to the ADA's first principle of nondiscrimination.

The fears about cost and difficulty for making materials available in alternative formats usually far exceed the reality. This is an area where even some of the benchmark companies need to expand their efforts.

Awareness Training for Recruiters

Recruiters are usually the company's first point of contact with job candidates, particularly for certain populations such as college seniors. The principle of "first impressions," discussed earlier, works both ways. If a recruiter commits a *faux pas* with a person with a disability, the consequences could include a formal legal action or the loss of the individual as an employment prospect. The people who are sent to recruit need to know how to avoid both of these undesirable consequences.

A number of organizations now provide "off the shelf" programs for awareness or sensitivity training. The best-known system, called "Windmills," has been used, quite effectively, by organizations across the country. Other training systems should be checked out very carefully before investing time and money. Many entrepreneurs who have presented themselves as ADA experts, even presuming to be "certified" ADA consultants, actually know very little about the ADA or employment of people with disabilities—*caveat emptor*. The best way to identify high-quality awareness trainers is to inquire at local or state organizations for people with disabilities. Call and ask for referrals.

Action Steps for the Recruiting Function

In summary, a few management actions can go a long way in moving an organization toward the goal of barrier-free recruiting:

- Examine the recruiting policies and practices to determine if any group of people with disabilities is categorically excluded.
- Train recruiters to understand basic facts about the major categories of disabilities and to respond properly to persons with disabilities.
- Promote a mind-set in recruiters that focuses upon abilities, not disabilities.
- Develop an inclusionary recruiting strategy that enables the organization to tap into the best sources for the best-qualified and highest quality employees.
- Provide a short checklist for recruiters' use to ensure that the recruiting site is accessible and that materials are available in alternative formats (e.g., audiotape).

Actions like these promote the ADA's first principle of nondiscrimination and move the organization toward the goal of fully integrating the ADA into routine human resource activities.

THE APPLICATION PROCESS

Every aspect of the application process should also be accessible. The rule of thumb can be put this way: If the individual can do the job, he or she should be able to apply for it. For example, if the job does not require reading, either because literacy is not required or because alternative accommodations can be used, a person should not have to read to apply for the position. This suggests that if a written application is required for a non-reading position, a viable candidate may be unnecessarily excluded. Some companies address this problem by offering all applicants the option of personal assistance with the application form.

The "Clean" Application Form

The best practice regarding job application forms under the ADA is actually quite simple:

Practice #8

Ask no disability- or health-related questions on employment applications.

This is what could be called a "clean" application form. Following are some examples of the kinds of questions you do *not* want on your application forms. (These examples were taken directly from actual job applications in use as recently as early 1992, immediately prior to the effective dates of the ADA's employment provisions.)

1. Any health problems or physical defects which could affect your employment? If any such health problems or defects exist, please explain.
2. Do you have any physical condition which may limit your ability to perform the job applied for or limit your ability to perform other jobs?
   Yes _____ No _____ If yes, please explain in detail the nature of the condition and how it may affect performance.
3. Do you have any physical or mental disability or illness which might limit your ability to perform the essential duties of the position you are seeking?
   No _____ Yes _____ If yes, describe.
   [Note: This *may* be acceptable, but only if the essential duties have been clearly described.]

4. Do you presently have any disability, medical condition, handicap, or disease that would prevent you from standing continually for periods up to five hours, lifting items up to 50 pounds, or obtaining a food handler's permit?
No _____ Yes _____ If yes, please explain.
5. Do you have any physical, mental, or medical impairments which would interfere with your ability to perform job-related functions?

Other examples of *inappropriate* questions (taken from EEOC materials) include:

6. Have you ever been treated for any of the following? (Followed by a checklist of conditions and diseases.)
7. Have you ever been hospitalized? If so, for what conditions?
8. How many days were you absent from work because of illness last year?
9. Are you taking any prescription drugs?
10. Have you ever been treated for drug addiction or alcoholism?
11. Have you ever been treated by a psychologist or psychiatrist?
12. Have you ever filed for workers' compensation insurance?

As these "bad" examples show, some major employers used inappropriate questions until quite recently. And a few of these companies may still be asking for the wrong information. The easiest way to fix this problem is with correction fluid—just white it out. For some organizations, this may require white-out in "the handy paragraph-size spray can," as the old joke goes. But as an easy, low-cost step toward compliance, few tactics match this one.

If you have applications on file with health or disability information on them, it would be wise to mask that information in some way at whatever point in time these individuals become job candidates so that the information cannot be used in a discriminatory way.

Under certain conditions, the application may include some questions that focus on the applicant's disability—or, more precisely, his/her *ability*:

- If (and only if) the applicant has been provided a specific job description or list of essential job functions, it is appropriate to ask the person whether he or she can do the functions with or without an accommodation. This question essentially gets at whether the person is actually qualified to do the job—a perfectly legitimate request in this case.
- If the applicant says that an accommodation will be necessary to do those essential functions, the employer may ask, either on the application or in an interview, how the person would perform the tasks and what accommodations would be needed. It is critical, however, that the information about the needed accommodation not be used in the hiring decision—a clear case of discrimination.

This discussion leads us back to the point where the purpose of the ADA and the purpose of good employment management converge: finding and hiring the best people for the job, focusing on the individual's abilities and the contribution he or she will make to the organization.

Application Availability and Dissemination

The same general guidelines apply to the application form as to job announcements. One very easy accommodation is simply to handle applications by mail; most firms do this anyway, but it can prevent a problem if the application office is not accessible.

Action Steps for the Application Process

In summary, a few management actions can help to ensure that the application process allows the organization to receive applications from qualified people with disabilities:

- Make sure that applications are available in accessible locations or by mail.
- Provide an alternative for those who are unable to complete a written application.
- Train staff who hand out and receive applications on proper ways to respond to people with disabilities.
- Clean up the application form to remove any health or disability questions, except when applicants are asked to explain how they will perform specifically identified essential job functions.

INTERVIEWING APPLICANTS

The interviewing process raises a number of issues. Interviewers may ask inappropriate questions or ask them in the wrong sequence. Faced with an applicant with an obvious disability, they may feel uncertain about how to broach the subject, if at all. Let's look at some of the most common problems.

Getting the Necessary Information

In any interview situation, a manager's prime concern is to identify the best-qualified candidate for a position, and that requires learning enough about the candidate to make an informed decision. When a manager overreacts to the ADA's limitations on interview questions, or becomes nervous about offending the individual with a disability, he or she may avoid asking those questions that would yield pertinent information.

Direct, relevant interview questions focused on the job or position should not be soft-pedaled or ignored. There is absolutely no discrimination involved in asking a candidate to describe qualifications, credentials, and experience related to the job. The management principle can be stated this way:

Practice #9

Maintain interview standards without compromise.

This management practice serves as a reminder that the ADA was not designed to alter the fundamental processes of employment, but to remove the discrimination that has infiltrated these processes.

The Sequence of Interview Questions

The sequence of questions is important, and an improper sequence can put a company at risk. Even the best companies have faced difficulties in trying to communicate this approach to line managers and supervisors who conduct job interviews. The best practice in interview sequencing can be stated in this way:

Practice #10

Establish the job requirements and the person's qualifications before discussing disability-related issues.

The interview is intended to help the interviewer know what an applicant *can* do, more so than what he or she *can't*. With this in mind, here is one appropriate interview sequence:

1. Review the essential functions and basic requirements of the position.

- Go over all the essential functions to ensure that the individual understands what abilities the position requires.
- Discuss any other requirements, such as attendance, number of hours, and schedule.

2. Discuss the candidate's experience, qualifications, and interests.

- Ask for specific experience and related information in precisely the same manner you would with any other candidate.
- Resist the temptation to raise the issue of an obvious or suspected disability.

3. Ask if he or she anticipates any difficulties doing the job.

- Request that the individual please be specific.
- If the individual notes a disability, give assurance of nondiscrimination.

4. Go through the reasonable accommodation process (see below, page 60).

5. Make closing comments, especially regarding the company policy of nondiscrimination.

- Follow the same procedures that you would with any other candidate.
- Reassure the candidate that the hiring decision will not be affected by the need for a reasonable accommodation.

Some HR experts recommend reversing the first two steps in the sequence to ease the transition between task and accommodation. Interviewers may certainly feel free to follow that pattern, recognizing the most important feature of the sequence, namely, that *the presentation of essential functions precedes any discussion of disability.*

Line managers and supervisors will have a better grasp of the importance of this seemingly subtle element if they keep focused on the ADA's first principle. The reason for the interview in the first place is to determine whether this individual can do the job and fit, effectively, into the organization's operations. Discussions about the person's disability are only relevant if it affects his or her ability to perform the job, or if the cost of accommodating will prove inordinate—things you will not know until you have discussed them. Based on sight alone, the interviewer can no more determine the job impact of the disability than he can guess the applicant's taste in food or music. The message to the interviewer: Don't jump to conclusions.

Approaching the Subject of an Obvious Disability

What should the interviewer do if a person being interviewed has an obvious disability, such as blindness, deafness, or a mobility impairment, that the interviewer believes may affect performance? First, focus on the ADA's "true north" and remember that nondiscrimination is the key. More than anything else, this compass reading helps the interviewer approach each individual one at a time, not leaping to conclusions or making false assumptions, but giving the candidate a chance to make his or her case for being hired.

An interviewer doesn't have to pretend not to notice the obvious. Timing and tact make the difference between an embarrassing blunder and a gracious handling of a sensitive issue. (For a listing of the types of questions that violate this principle, see Exhibit 2.4; for guidelines on etiquette, see Exhibit 2.5.) If the candidate does not bring it up during the interview, follow the sequence described earlier. If the interviewer believes the disability may have a direct effect on job performance, he or she can raise the issues, as in these examples:

- A blind person is being interviewed for a data entry position. The interviewer could ask the candidate to describe how she would do the essential function of taking data from printed log sheets and entering them into the computer. The candidate would need to demonstrate or explain how she could do this function without being able to read the log sheets. Note: This can be done without any reference to disability.

Exhibit 2.4. Some things not to say or do in interviewing persons with disabilities.

SOME THINGS *NOT* TO SAY OR TALK ABOUT

1. "One of my best friends is [handicapped, blind, deaf, etc.]."
2. These words: "handicapped" (use "disabled" or "person with a disability"); "gimp," "cripple."
3. References to Tiny Tim, poster children, circus people, Ray Charles (or any other disabled celebrity), Special Olympics.
4. The term "wheelchair bound" (use "wheelchair user").
5. Generalizations about persons with disabilities (e.g., "Handicapped people usually work harder than others").
6. General discussions about the "challenges" disabled people face.
7. "You didn't sound handicapped over the phone."
8. "My mother (grandmother, etc.) was in a wheelchair."

SOME THINGS *NOT* TO DO

1. Speak louder to a blind person.
2. Speak slower or louder to a deaf person who is using an interpreter.
3. Use a condescending or patronizing tone of voice.
4. Offer to have someone carry a wheelchair user into a non-accessible site.
5. Make too much of the minor accommodations involved in the interview (e.g., making a scene of moving a chair away from a table to accommodate a wheelchair user).
6. Offer more than the normal courtesies afforded candidates.
7. Stare at the part of the person's body that is disabled.
8. Tell "handicap jokes" (Helen Keller, etc.).

- A wheelchair user with a driver's license and direct experience applies for a position as a small package delivery driver. The interviewer could ask how he will perform the required tasks in the company van. The candidate might then explain, for example, that the company could either

(*Text continues on p. 60*)

Exhibit 2.5.   Disability etiquette.

Some general considerations . . .

- People with disabilities are entitled to the courtesies that you extend to anyone. This includes their personal privacy. If you don't generally ask people about their sex lives, or their complexions, or their incomes, then don't ask people with disabilities about theirs.
- If you don't make a habit of leaning or hanging on to people you're with, then don't lean or hang on someone's wheelchair. Wheelchairs are an extension of personal space for people who use them.
- When you offer to assist someone with a vision impairment, allow the person to take your arm. This will help you to guide, rather than propel or lead this person.
- Treat adults as adults. Call a person by his or her first name only when you're extending this familiarity to everyone present. Don't patronize people who use wheelchairs by patting them on the head. Reserve this sign of affection for children, even if a wheelchair user's head rests temptingly at about the same height as a child's.

In conversation . . .

- When talking with someone who has a disability, speak directly to that person rather than through a companion who may be along.
- Relax. Don't be embarrassed if you happen to use accepted, common expressions, such as "See you later" or "Got to be running along," that seem to relate to the person's disability.
- To get the attention of a person who has a hearing disability, tap the person on the shoulder or wave your hand. Look directly at the person and speak clearly, slowly, and expressively to establish if the person can read your lips. Not all persons with hearing impairments can lip-read. Those who do will rely on facial expressions and body language to help in understanding. Show consideration by placing yourself facing

the light source and keeping hands and food away from your mouth when speaking. Shouting won't help. Written notes will.

- When talking with a person in a wheelchair for more than a few minutes, place yourself at the wheelchair user's eye level to spare both of you a stiff neck.
- When greeting a person with a severe loss of vision, always identify yourself and others who may be with you. When conversing in a group, remember to say the name of the person to whom you are speaking to give a vocal cue. Speak in a normal tone of voice, indicate when you move from one place to another, and let it be known when the conversation is at an end.
- Give whole, unhurried attention when you're talking to a person who has difficulty speaking. Keep your manner encouraging rather than correcting, be patient rather than speak for the person. When necessary, ask short questions that require short answers or a nod or shake of the head. Never pretend to understand if you are having difficulty doing so. Repeat what you understand. The person's reaction will clue you in and guide you to understanding.

Some common courtesies . . .

- Offer assistance to a person with a disability if you feel like it, but wait until your offer is accepted BEFORE you help, and listen to any instructions the person may want to give.
- When giving directions to a person in a wheelchair, consider distance, weather conditions, and physical obstacles such as stairs, curbs, and steep hills.
- Use specifics such as "left a hundred feet" or "right two yards" when directing a person with a visual impairment.
- Be considerate of the extra time it might take for a person with a disability to get things done or said. Let the person set the pace in walking and talking.
- When planning events involving persons with disabilities, consider their needs ahead of time. If an insurmountable barrier exists, let them know about it prior to the event.

Source: "Awareness Is the First Step Toward Change," National Easter Seal Society. Used by permission.

modify its van for his use, or pay him a mileage allowance to use his personal vehicle (which is already modified). Having learned that the applicant is in fact qualified to do the job with an accommodation, the company could determine whether either accommodation was reasonable under the ADA.

These examples demonstrate the kind of circumstances in which a known disability can trigger an appropriate question about the individual's ability to perform essential job functions. They also show that the interviewer's perception that a problem might exist does not mean the problem is insurmountable. In the case of the van driver, the first accommodation (to modify the company van) may be reasonable for larger companies, and the second (to use his own vehicle) might well be reasonable for a company of any size.

Presenting the Company Policy of Nondiscrimination

Every organization covered under the ADA (employers with 25 or more employees now, with 15 or more after July 26, 1994) should have a written policy of nondiscrimination on the basis of disability. The policy should follow the essential provisions of the ADA, including guarantees of nondiscrimination in all aspects of the employment process, both pre- and post-employment.

For a sample nondiscrimination policy, see Exhibit 2.6.

THE REASONABLE ACCOMMODATION PROCESS

The concept of "reasonable accommodation" has been the focus of much of the concern about the ADA's elusive requirements—it just does not readily lend itself to quantification or absolute, objective standards. And yet, from a management perspective, the concept can have tremendous value because it allows for great flexibility in making appropriate case-by-case management decisions. When the idea of reasonable accommodation captures a manager's thinking, it can change from an elusive nuisance to a useful analytical tool, particularly within the context of the overarching principle of the ADA, to eliminate discrimination against people with disabilities.

Whether the accommodation relates to a new hire, as we are focusing on in this chapter, or a current employee (discussed in the next chapter), the process is fundamentally the same. The four steps in the process, as laid out in the EEOC regulations, are:

1. *Look at the particular job involved. Determine its purpose and its essential functions.* This is the process discussed in Chapter 1 regarding job analysis and development of a job or position description.
2. *Consult with the individual with a disability to find out his or her specific physical or mental abilities and limitations.* This refers, of course, to those abilities related to the essential functions.
3. *In consultation with the individual, identify potential accommodations and assess the effectiveness of each.* Note that this step has two key elements: the dialogue with the individual and the assessment of the effectiveness of potential accommodations.
4. *Considering the individual's preference, select the accommodation that best serves the needs of the individual and the employer.* The goal is to maximize the value to both parties.

The process, then, is fairly straightforward.

What is meant by an "accommodation"? The ADA offers several examples of categories of accommodations to consider:

1. *Making facilities accessible.* Not every facility or office in the company must be accessible, but those to be used by persons with disabilities should be, where practicable.
2. *Job restructuring.* If a position currently involves multiple tasks, one or more of which the person with a disability

Exhibit 2.6. Sample nondiscrimination policy.

Our organization is an equal opportunity employer, and our corporate policy is not to discriminate against any individual on the basis of race, ethnicity, color, creed, sex, marital status, age, national origin, physical or mental disability, or any other basis prohibited by federal, state or local law. We are committed to the principle that employment decisions should be based on merit alone, and forbid unlawful discrimination by any manager, supervisor, or other employee.

In response to the Americans with Disabilities Act and related state and local laws, we provide reasonable accommodations to qualified individuals with disabilities, and do not permit the provision of such an accommodation to be a factor in an employment action, unless the accommodation poses an undue hardship or a direct threat to health and safety (that is, a significant risk of substantial harm), or if a clear business necessity warrants special consideration.

Optional Paragraph: [We follow federal guidelines in the process of identifying and providing reasonable accommodations for employees who require them to perform the essential functions of their jobs. The process is interactive, involving the employee and his/her supervisor, human resource department staff, and others, as appropriate. We give priority to the accommodation desired by the employee, and will provide reasonable accommodations necessary for effective performance of the job's essential functions, unless constrained by an undue hardship or other considerations permitted by law. The employee needing an accommodation has the responsibility to initiate the request for the accommodation, by discussing the need with a supervisor or human resource staff person.]

Employees who believe that they have experienced unlawful discrimination should submit a written complaint to the human resources department/EEO coordinator at the time of the action or as soon as possible thereafter. The complaint should describe as specifically as possible what happened and give the names of the individuals involved, dates and times of the events, a full description of what was said or done and by whom. If there were any witnesses, their names should also be provided. Regardless of the outcome of the matter, we will not retaliate against an employee for filing a complaint.

As soon as possible after the complaint is received, we will investigate the complaint and try to resolve the matter. If we believe unlawful discrimination took place, we will take appropriate action against the offending person, and will notify the offended person of the action, as far as can be done without violating any person's rights to privacy. We will also remedy any loss to the offended person resulting from the discrimination.

---

      could not do, these tasks could be reassigned to another person, perhaps in exchange for other duties currently being performed by someone else.

3. *Part-time or modified work schedules.* Examples include making one full-time position into two part-time slots ("job sharing") and using flex-time.

4. *Reassignment to a vacant position.* This applies principally to current employees who become disabled.

5. *Special equipment or devices.* Examples range from very simple and inexpensive devices like magnifying glasses and tools for reaching, to highly sophisticated electronic equipment.

6. *Administrative adjustments.* Procedures for, say, punching a time clock that is in an inaccessible location, or filling out printed reporting forms that a blind person could not see, could be modified without eliminating the activity or thwarting its purpose.

7. *Providing support staff.* Particularly in larger firms or with other firms on an occasional basis, the provision of readers or interpreters may be reasonable.

These categories should all be put on the table for consideration. Other kinds of accommodations are possible; the key is to be creative and to recognize that each individual is unique.

After determining that (1) an accommodation is needed for an ADA-covered disability, and (2) that one or more accommodations is available, the next step is to determine whether the accommodations are reasonable. At this point, it may be useful to remember the statistics we offered in the introduction: Most accommodations are very reasonable—by any standard. The most frequently requested accommodation—a flexible work schedule—normally costs little or nothing.

The process for determining "reasonableness" involves consideration of several factors:

1. *The nature and cost of the accommodation.* Accommodations that require little or no effort by the employer and involve little or no cost would almost always be reasonable. For other accommodations, the firm can consider the extent of the impact, financially and otherwise.

2. *The overall financial resources of the facility.* Even if an office or site is part of a larger company, the effect of the cost of the accommodation on the company's resources may be taken into account. For example, if a chain retailer has a store in a small town, and that store is just managing to keep its doors open, an expensive accommodation could put the store in such a financially troubled position that the parent company would have a difficult time justifying its continued operation.

3. *The financial resources of the "covered entity."* In the chain store example mentioned above, this factor refers to the parent company. If this chain retailer is substantially profitable and therefore able to assume the cost of an accommodation for the local store, this changes the baseline for consideration of what constitutes an undue financial hardship.

4. *The type of operation of the business.* This is something of a catch-all category, including management structure, workforce composition, and the relationship of the local operation to the parent company. Examples of considerations in this category include whether the accommodation would require the operation to substantially modify its overall management structure or institute burdensome administrative procedures.

Each organization will need to make some decisions about what constitutes an "undue burden" based upon its unique circumstances. Some companies have decided on a total annual amount they will set aside as an accommodations "pool," based on a judgment of what is "reasonable" and what would constitute an "undue hardship." Once those funds have been spent, the firm will not make additional accommodations.

Other firms have taken a less rigid approach. For example, one fairly large and decentralized company has set a $350 limit on accommodations that each of its field offices can make at their discretion. Accommodations whose costs exceed that amount are referred to the headquarters office designated as having the ADA compliance oversight responsibility. Two important ideas come from this approach: (1) each office can make its own decisions on the vast majority of accommodations without being concerned with making assessments of reasonableness—if they are under the limit, they are reasonable; and (2) higher cost accommodations can be more rapidly considered in light of the overall corporate resources, and can also be reviewed by the corporate expert in making accommodations for people with disabilities.

For additional information on reasonable accommodation, as well as examples of successful accommodations, see Appendix A.

PRE-EMPLOYMENT TESTING

As a basic management strategy, employers test candidates for certain positions to help identify the best candidate. If the test contains a significant bias, whether explicit or hidden, the effect of the test will be to screen out some good candidates, perhaps the best one, and good managers want no part of it. Test design has now reached a level of sophistication that reduces or eliminates much of this bias. If a test does not pass muster on its validity as an instrument, it will not serve the employer well.

The ADA's attention to pre-employment testing follows this

same principle of good management relative to people with disabilities. If a test, or the conditions of its administration, tends to screen out a qualified candidate because of his or her disability, then it does not serve the interests of the employer or the candidate. Some of the considerations from the ADA point of view are that:

- The test should be directly related to the position for which the individual is applying OR based on clear business necessity. In other words, there should be a good reason for giving the test, directly related to an appropriate hiring decision.
- The test should be administered under nondiscriminatory conditions in such areas as the location and arrangement of the test site, the method of administration (pencil and paper, oral, etc.), and time given. Examples of accommodations that can be used in this area are discussed below.
- A test should only test the knowledge or skills and abilities required for essential job functions. For example, if reading is not required as an essential function, a test requiring reading could screen out a qualified candidate who simply cannot read or read well.
- The test should be given to all (qualified) candidates for that position, regardless of disability. Managers should not have discretion to decide if and when a candidate needs to be tested; it is a case of all or none.

Examples of Appropriate and Inappropriate Tests

First, let us consider two examples that address the issue of whether the test measures qualities and abilities that are directly related to the essential functions of the job:

Example 1: A functional literacy test given to applicants for a variety of positions.

This test would be appropriate if a specific job required that the person be able to read and write to perform the essential functions. However, if a reasonable alternative to reading or writing could be used, such as audiotaped instructions or visual symbols, the pencil and paper literacy test may not be appropriate.

Example 2: A personality test given to candidates for a position known to be highly stressful; the test attempts to measure the person's ability to handle the stress.

The function of the test appears to satisfy the criterion that the test be job-related. However, if the test also measures other psychological traits, such as the presence of latent personality disorders, these results would likely be inappropriate to use in a hiring decision.

In the next examples, the question is whether there is a clear reason to give the test based on business necessity.

Example 1: A basic math skills test, given to individuals applying for an assembly line position.

Workers must make periodic adjustments to the process, and this requires simple mathematical calculations. A computer normally does the calculations, but the employee must be able to do the calculations if the computer malfunctions. The reasonable alternative would appear to be a pocket calculator. However, if the company believes that there is significant risk even with this device, the test may be justified on the basis of business necessity, i.e., to avoid risk of major quality problems. This risk should be documented, with supporting evidence.

Example 2: A test to determine an individual's ability to perform work at home.

An applicant with a disability has asked for the reasonable accommodation of working at home for a certain number of days each week or month because of the transportation problems he faces. The company wishes to determine whether the individual has enough initiative to do this productively, and gives the person a test to make that determination. This test would probably violate the ADA unless the company can show that the history of such working arrangements has been extremely poor and that there is a business necessity to minimize the loss. Moreover, the firm may also need to show that the supervisor's ability to promote and monitor performance on those days is substantially limited.

A quick "reality check" of tests being used could help to identify problem areas.

Examples of Testing Accommodations

EEOC has provided this list of possible alternative test formats and accommodations:

- Substituting a written test for an oral test (or written instructions for oral instructions) for people with impaired speaking or hearing skills;
- Administering the test in large print, in Braille, by a reader, or on a computer for people with visual or other reading disabilities;
- Allowing people with visual or learning disabilities or who have limited use of their hands to record test answers by tape recorder, dictation, or computer;
- Providing extra time to complete a test for people with certain learning disabilities or impaired writing skills;
- Simplifying test language for people who have limited language skills because of a disability;
- Scheduling rest breaks for people with mental and other disabilities that require such relief;
- Assuring that a test site is accessible to a person with a mobility disability;
- Allowing a person to take a test in a separate room, if that person's mental disability prevents him or her from performing well if there are distractions. (This assumes that work in a group setting is not relevant to the job.)

- Where it is not possible to test an individual with a disability in an alternative format, an employer may be required, as a reasonable accommodation, to evaluate the skill or ability being tested through some other means, such as an interview, education, work experience, licenses or certification, or a job demonstration for a trial period.

These categories and types of accommodations make sense when viewed in the light of the ADA's first principle. The goal is not to give special treatment but to remove disability-related barriers to equal employment opportunity.

Medical Tests

The guidelines for thinking about medical testing also apply the principle of nondiscrimination.

1. Medical examinations that are given prior to an offer of employment are not allowed under the ADA.
2. However, medical examinations may be given *after* an offer of employment has been made if the examinations meet the following criteria:
   a) All employees coming into the particular job are required to take the same kind of medical exam;
   b) The results are kept confidential and retained in a separate set of files, away from the general personnel files; and
   c) The examination results are not used to deny an individual with disabilities the position *unless* the exam reveals a condition that prevents the person from performing the essential functions of the job with or without a reasonable accommodation.
3. In general, required medical exams should be related to the essential functions of the job and have a clear business necessity.
4. Post-employment medical exams may be given on a voluntary basis, but under the same confidentiality arrange-

ment and nondiscrimination provisions as post-offer exams.

5. Before an individual is denied a position for medical reasons, it is advisable to have a doctor review the job description (focusing on the essential functions) and identify which essential function(s) the person is unable to perform for health or medical reasons.

Why does the ADA limit such a potentially important activity as pre-employment medical examinations? As the "true north" principle of nondiscrimination and good management suggest, managers do not want to risk losing a qualified, high-quality candidate simply because the person has a disability or medical condition.

The first court case filed under the ADA illustrates the issue well. A company learned that an employee had cancer and decided to terminate his employment for that reason. EEOC is charging that the firm based its decision to terminate on the basis of false assumptions about the individual's ability to perform the essential job functions. According to EEOC, the man's cancer does not limit his ability to work in his current position. The case points to the dangers of false assumptions or inferences from medical information.

Actions

Some actions that can be taken to ensure that pre-employment testing practices do not screen out qualified candidates simply because they have disabilities:

- Review the employment tests being used in order to determine if each one meets the ADA criteria for an appropriate test.
- Put tests into alternative formats to the greatest degree reasonable.
- Train test administrators to respond properly to testing situations involving persons with disabilities.
- Ensure that the use of test results does not discriminate.

One note on the final point: Even if the test has been conducted under nondiscriminatory circumstances, the results should not be handled in a discriminatory way. For example, if a manager can see that a test was administered using an alternative format, he or she may use this fact to draw unnecessary and inappropriate inferences about the individual's ability to perform the job. It will be important to ensure that the ADA's first principle remains foremost with managers and supervisors, and that they are sensitive to disability issues in their use of test data.

HIRING DECISIONS

The compass of the ADA, as we have said, has its "true north" in the principle that people with disabilities should not be discriminated against in any aspect of the employment process. This principle of nondiscrimination is absolutely *not* affirmative action, but equal opportunity. For employee selection, implementation of the ADA in no way implies the use of hiring quotas. Rather, the goal is to ensure that people with disabilities who are qualified for the job are not denied the position for any disability-related reason.

Best practices in employee selection do, however, finally result in employment of people with disabilities, leading to our next "best practice":

Practice #11

Hire people with disabilities.

At the time of this writing, very few companies are doing any hiring at all, so this benchmark may not have much immediate opportunity to be tested. This fact, that more individuals are being laid off than hired, may help to explain why, in the first three months of ADA implementation, more than 40 percent of complaints filed with the EEOC under the ADA have been for *discharge*-related discrimination.

Eventually, most companies will return to a hiring phase.

And it is this phase that puts a company's commitment to effective ADA implementation to the acid test. The best companies not only work to eliminate formal barriers to employment, such as discriminatory employment policies and procedures, but also address the issue of whether their efforts culminate in nondiscriminatory hiring decisions. Following the "maps" of ADA compliance will not work if managers are not oriented to "true north."

One way to measure an organization's status relative to this benchmark is for HR staff to debrief managers who have made hiring decisions.

- Were any viable candidates people with disabilities? If not, were there any barriers to their applying for the position—barriers that need to removed?
- If qualified candidates with disabilities did apply, was the reason for denying them the job disability-related? If so, did the company properly follow the reasonable accommodation process and come to the right conclusion about "undue hardship"?
- Are the managers aware of any attitudinal issues that could have affected the decision? Did any myths or stereotypes, false assumptions about abilities or disabilities, or fears about the impact on other employees come into play?

Focus on Ability, not Disability

The ADA was designed to permit employers to make their own hiring decisions, using appropriate standards and judgments, as long as those decisions did not discriminate. As we have said several times throughout this briefing, each decision must be made as a separate action, with accommodations for people with disabilities made on a case-by-case basis.

At the heart of this approach is the assumption that employers should, and will, make hiring decisions on the basis of ability, not disability. The best companies take this standard as a given.

DEALING WITH THE INTANGIBLES

Sometimes managers who have the responsibility for a hiring decision find need to consider more than a candidate's credentials. Other, less tangible, considerations come into play. For example:

- How will this individual fit in with the rest of the staff?
- Will her/his presence affect morale, either positively or negatively?
- Does this person share the values of our corporate culture?

These and other similar concerns can become extremely important when deciding between two close candidates; thus, the concerns are a valid part of the decision-making process.

The intangibles become problematic under the ADA at the point where they relate to the person's disability. The problem of attitudes can be significant if, for example, co-workers feel uncomfortable around the person with a disability. But this is one instance where staff at all levels need to know that the ADA *is* a civil rights law. As such, it protects a particular class of individuals from discrimination, regardless of whether that discrimination results from the presence of myths and stereotypes, false assumptions, or blatant discriminatory attitudes.

A comparison with other protected classes may be helpful here. The arguments about "people feeling uncomfortable" were once brought forward to argue against racially integrated housing, restaurants, social clubs, swimming pools, and water fountains.

It may be useful to try an approach that one organization uses in its training programs: Substitute "blacks" or "women" into statements that are sometimes made about people with disabilities to see how the analogy works. For example, "We couldn't hire _____ here because they wouldn't fit in." Or, "I don't know any _____ who could do this job."

We know not to make such generalizations about racial or ethnic minorities and women, but many are still learning about people with disabilities in this respect (pun intended).

3

Managing Employees with Disabilities

According to the ADA, employers have an obligation to ensure that employees with disabilities can enjoy all the benefits and privileges of employment, unless it would impose an undue hardship to do so. From the management perspective, the ADA merely codifies for a particular group of people what the best-managed companies have always known: Acknowledging and responding to the diverse needs and interests of their employees pay off in the bottom line. An employee who becomes disabled has experience that should not be lost.

The standard-bearers in employment of people with disabilities include firms like IBM, Marriott, Hewlett-Packard, and others with a strong track record in all aspects of employment. When they hire a person with a disability, the accommodations for that person are, in most cases, simple variations on their practices with employees who do not have disabilities. Whether they offer (as many firms now do) flex-time, cafeteria benefits programs, day care programs, parental leave, fitness facilities, or other incentives, the desired goal is to hire and keep good people.

Weak employment conditions may tempt line managers to be less responsive to employee needs. That view, as most HR managers well know, is shortsighted and ultimately counterproductive. Long-term employment projections continue to suggest that skilled and competent employees will be in great demand for years to come. People with disabilities will be an increasing part of the overall mix of diverse people at the core of successful businesses. A limited view of the benefits of effectively employing people with disabilities will cause some firms to miss the opportunity presented by the ADA.

This chapter looks at what happens *after* the hiring decision, and includes discussion of how to deal with currently employed individuals who become disabled. As a reminder, all the discussions of these issues have as their underlying theme the fundamental notion of nondiscrimination—the "true north" of the ADA compass. Each organization, and each unique management system and style must be oriented toward that compass point and then, within the relatively broad parameters of the ADA regulations, develop and follow its own maps. If individuals at every level within the organization can keep their focus on that first principle, many of the details will take care of themselves.

Human resource managers will be most effective in the role of catalysts for change. By working with senior managers to increase their awareness of the need and importance for ADA leadership from the top, and by helping to disseminate information and promote awareness about the ADA throughout the entire organization, the HR staff can be the ADA gatekeepers. The material within this briefing can be adapted and used toward that end.

SUPERVISORY STRATEGIES

Supervision of employees with disabilities is, in most cases, no different from supervision of non-disabled employees. This, of course, varies with the degree and type of the employee's disability. From a management perspective, the main concern is productivity, and the key considerations are identical to those for other employees:

- Does the individual have the tools, equipment, and work space needed to perform productively? What changes should be made to enhance his/her ability to perform at the highest possible level?
- Has he or she been adequately trained in the requirements of the position? What additional training will be needed, immediately and in the future?
- Are the performance standards and job expectations clear to both the employee and the supervisor? Have performance measures and evaluation processes been established to assess objectively the employee's performance on the essential job functions and determine where improvement is needed?
- Are there any interpersonal dynamics that may inhibit performance by the individual or his/her co-workers? Is any training or discussion needed to address problems in this area?

We will examine each of these areas from the perspective of the ADA's first principle and the concerns of a high-quality human resource management program.

Our discussion is built on the assumption that accommodating employees with disabilities is a subset of overall supervision, not a separate category. In other words, companies should not isolate employment concerns related to people with disabilities into some kind of separate management function. It may be useful to delegate primary responsibility for overseeing accommodations to an individual with that expertise, as Wells Fargo Bank and others have done. But the accommodation process needs to become fully integrated into the overall management of the organization. The "best practice" management approach to effective supervision of people with disabilities can be said this way:

Practice # 12

Make accommodating employees with disabilities a routine part of the process of empowering employees and enhancing their productivity.

The key here is to see people with disabilities in the larger context of the daily adjustments managers make to optimize employee productivity and satisfaction.

Dialogue Between Staff and Employees with Disabilities

The most basic element here, as with all employees, is open, direct, and appropriate communication. Many employers seem to be afraid of discussing the same management issues with employees with disabilities that they would discuss freely with others. This can be attributed, at least in part, to myths and stereotypes or to lack of experience in working with people with disabilities. In some cases, the problem may stem from fear of a formal complaint or other legal action.

Leadership from upper management and hands-on training from HR staff can reduce or eliminate many of these concerns. The benchmark companies have created environments that encourage open dialogue and emphasize the value of finding solutions through constructive interaction. The concept is a "win-win" transaction: for the employer, who desires to have productive people, and the employee, who wants to be able to work efficiently and productively without complications caused by the lack of a needed accommodation.

Discussions about accommodations normally take place for new employees in the context of the interview, as discussed in the previous chapter. Once the hiring decision has been made, the employer and employee should, ideally, develop an understanding that either one may initiate a discussion about adjustments or accommodations that could enhance productivity. This understanding has become the hallmark of good management in the 1990s—for *all* employees, not just people with disabilities.

MAKING REASONABLE ACCOMMODATIONS

When an employee becomes disabled, or when an individual comes forward to identify an existing disability that may need an accommodation, the process of determining a reasonable accommodation begins. The process will ultimately answer the first fundamental question we raised earlier:

- Does the individual have the tools, equipment, and work space needed to perform productively? What changes should be made to enhance his/her ability to perform at the highest possible level?

Let's review the process of determining a reasonable accommodation, as presented in Chapter 2.

1. *Look at the particular job involved. Determine its purpose and its essential functions.* This is the process discussed in Chapter 1 regarding job analysis and development of a job or position description.
2. *Consult with the individual to find out his or her specific physical or mental abilities and limitations.* This refers, of course, to those abilities related to the essential functions.
3. *In consultation with the individual, identify potential accommodations and assess the effectiveness of each.* Note that this step has two key elements: the dialogue with the individual and the assessment of the effectiveness of potential accommodations.
4. *Considering the individual's preference, select the accommodation that best serves the needs of the employee and the employer.* The goal is to maximize the value to both parties.

Each step should involve the effective application of the ADA's first principle of nondiscrimination, as well as good management. We will look at the critical elements of each step—in some detail—to identify how the parties involved can make the process work most productively.

Step 1: Job Analysis

Recall, from Chapter 1, that the reasonable accommodation process begins with the job to be done. While that should seem patently clear, the point is that the employer need not create a different job just for this individual (although in certain instances that may be warranted). Neither does the employer need to start by asking the individual a question like, "Which parts of the job can you do and which can you not do?" Rather, start with the job's essential functions as given and continue the process from there.

Step 2: Talk with the Individual

As we noted earlier, some managers feel they have to walk on eggshells, avoiding disability-related issues altogether. In some respects, that probably reflects an important intermediate stage on the way to the desired point of free communication: Better to be careful than to risk asking inappropriate or insensitive questions, as is done in far too many instances.

But EEOC has rightly said (and the best companies know) that unless the manager talks with the person with a disability, the decision about whether or how to make an accommodation will be made in ignorance—and will probably be wrong. False assumptions have led to many a business problem, and the purpose of this step is to prevent this from happening.

The individual with a disability bears the responsibility of telling the employer about any impact the disability will have on his or her ability to perform the essential job functions. The employer should not be forced to guess. (Reasonable accommodations are required only for known disabilities.) Nor should the employer probe into areas that do not bear directly on performance of the job, no matter how tempting it may become to do so. The process involves looking at each essential job function and asking the person with a disability whether she or he anticipates any difficulty doing that function, or whether an accommodation would enable the individual to do the job more effectively. If the person says no, that should end the inquiry on that function (unless there is strongly compelling evidence to the contrary).

Step 3: Identifying and Assessing Possible Accommodations

In most cases where an accommodation is needed, several options will be available. For example, a research analyst with very low vision (not blind) cannot read standard text because it is too small. Accommodation options could include a magnifying device, a computer that shows very large print on the screen and/or gives simulated voice readouts, or a personal reader. The first option would be low cost, but inefficient for large documents, thus reducing the individual's productivity. The second option could require a substantial up-front investment, but would be very efficient for the individual. The third option would not involve great initial expense, but would have a high long-term cost in wages and related costs.

From the employer's point of view, the decision could become a straightforward trade-off analysis: cost versus productivity. For the person with a disability, other factors could come into play. For some individuals, having a personal reader would be very desirable; for others, not desirable at all because of the relationship dynamics being introduced. The low-cost/low-productivity magnifier option could lead to very low job satisfaction levels for some; others might enjoy the more moderate pace. The computer could be very exciting for some, while completely threatening for someone who is "technophobic."

The assessment of the possible accommodations should be done through what EEOC calls an "informed interactive process" between the employer and the employee. As with most aspects of the ADA, the "case-by-case" approach is fundamental. Some companies have created a simple matrix with a place to list possible accommodations and the pros and cons of each. This tool can serve two purposes: (1) it can ensure that both the employer and the individual with a disability agree on the set of possible accommodations; and (2) it will provide a written record of the process. Both factors have merit, even when the discussion is being handled informally.

Step 4: Selecting the Accommodation

It may be that none of the possible accommodations is "reasonable" for the company to consider, because of cost or other "undue hardship." In that case, the employer needs to give the employee the option of providing the accommodation at his or her own expense, or identifying a government or philanthropic program to provide the needed equipment or other accommodation. This step should not be overlooked; it may help to gain the organization a valued employee even when the corporate resources are limited. Options to consider when the accommodation really is too expensive (and not unless this is the case) include state and local rehabilitation programs and organizations. The best source for these names is normally the state department of rehabilitation or the Governor's committee for employment of people with disabilities.

The primary consideration in selecting the accommodation is the preference of the individual with a disability. Managers are increasingly coming to recognize that when employees are empowered to make choices regarding their own worklife, they tend to be more satisfied and productive. As William Byham of Development Dimensions International put it, "Many organizations have accepted the link between empowerment and quality, customer service and productivity." When the "customer" is the employee with a disability, giving that individual the opportunity to have a say in a decision with such direct, personal impact will pay off in productivity over the long term.

Also, a well-intentioned manager may believe that the company should go for the more expensive accommodation (thus showing that the firm "wants the best" for its employees), when in fact the person with a disability actually prefers a lower cost accommodation. It should be noted, however, that, while the employee's preference is primary, the employer is not required to supply the accommodation of the employee's choice to the extent that doing so would create an undue hardship.

The best practice in making reasonable accommodations follows from this process:

Practice # 13

Create a "win-win" situation for the employer and the employee with a disability through the accommodation selected.

Discussion between the employer and the employee is important, in that it brings the concerns and feelings of both parties into the open, building the framework for the best possible decision. Both the employer's and the employee's perspectives need to be taken into account. As a vital concept of good management, the "win-win" approach embedded in the reasonable accommodation process works on the premise that satisfied employees contribute to corporate productivity goals.

TRAINING

The second basic supervisory question we raised early in this chapter concerned training needs:

- Has the person with a disability been adequately trained in the requirements of the position? What additional training will be needed, immediately and in the future?

Depending on the position, the training could range from a one-time effort in elementary tasks and procedures or a career-long process of management development or professional growth. This aspect of employment should be incorporated into the work experience of people with disabilities in the same way as it is with others.

The Barrier of the "Career Ladder"

For a wheelchair user, a ladder is no help at all. In some organizations, the obstacles to career advancement for people with disabilities are just as formidable as if they were rungs on a real ladder. This is true not only for wheelchair users, but for people with all kinds of disabilities. The career "ceilings" (and "walls") that other groups (minorities, women) have encountered, and arguably not resolved, are no less real for people with disabilities. The need is for a greater awareness of the potential contribution all kinds of people can make to the organization's effectiveness, and a more concerted effort to make those accommodations that will open up career opportunities.

In the area of training and development, the first and most critical consideration is that people with disabilities be provided full and equal access to the opportunities these activities present. The ADA's first principle makes this notion a "given," but actions need to follow to make it a reality.

Accessible Sites

By now, most HR managers know the importance of holding all employment activities, including training, in physically accessible sites. If the organization typically uses an inaccessible site, whether its own or another, selection of a new site or modifying the existing one should be pursued as soon as possible, even if the organization has no one currently on staff who needs the accessibility features. This may prevent a management crisis in the event that a new hire has a disability or a current employee becomes disabled.

Accessibility includes more than providing for wheelchair use, although ramping and other modifications for wheelchair users tend to be the most expensive and difficult. Consider also (1) tactile signage (especially for restrooms and elevators) for people who are blind or visually impaired; (2) assistive listening devices for people who are hard of hearing (not deaf); and (3) smooth walking surfaces for people who use wheelchairs, canes, or walkers. These are a few examples of the kinds of modifications that may need to be made.

Program Modifications

As much as possible, every aspect of a training program should be accessible for employees with disabilities. Both the ADA and good management require it. The modifications to enable this to occur will vary with each person with a disability and each kind of training program. For example, training videos should be open-captioned for employees with hearing impairments (others find it useful as well); large print, audiotape, or Braille versions of training materials should be prepared for individuals with vision impairments, depending on the nature of the impairment and the person's preferred method of receiving the materials; audiotape versions of materials, graphic symbols (vs. text), and additional learning time can be accommodations for people with certain kinds of learning disabilities or mental retardation. The ADA's case-by-case analysis should be applied here.

PERFORMANCE EVALUATION

The principle of nondiscrimination on the basis of disability ("true north") under the ADA suggests that performance evaluations for people with disabilities will not be conducted any differently from those of other employees. The questions we raised in the beginning of this section regarding performance of all employees were:

- Are the performance standards and job expectations clear to both the employee and the supervisor? Have performance measures and evaluation processes been established to assess objectively the employee's performance on the essential job functions and determine where improvement is needed?

The development of objective standards for performance evaluation can serve to remove some of the potential for discrimination.

Discrimination can creep into the process in several ways:

- The central concern we have expressed throughout this briefing is the issue of attitudes. Supervisors can have inaccurate or inappropriate ideas about the performance of people with disabilities. For example, sometimes expectations are too low (the "poor thing" attitude) or too high (people with disabilities as over-achievers).
- Another attitudinal issue has to do with basic prejudice. Hopefully this will not be common, but it is important to recognize that it is real and present in the workplace. Without clear, objective performance standards, this problem can more readily surface.
- If performance criteria do not relate to the essential functions of the job, the evaluation may examine marginal or nonessential functions and result in an unfair and discriminatory evaluation.

A form to "evaluate the evaluation" can be helpful as a periodic ADA review activity. Many different questions could be asked on such a form to help determine whether discrimination of this kind has occurred or is likely to occur. The five issues that follow will be considered as examples of areas where the manager or supervisor could go awry in the performance evaluation. Although this list is not exhaustive, it may help to focus thinking on the implications of the ADA for performance evaluations.

1. *Does the evaluation measure only those performance elements related to the essential functions of the job?* For example, the evaluation might include questions about performance of non-

essential or marginal functions. If the person with a disability could not do those functions or not do them well, his or her evaluation could be lowered unfairly for disability-related reasons.

2. *Are evaluation factors presented in terms of the job tasks and responsibilities?* General performance measures such as "is a team player" or "works hard" have some value to an organization, but may interfere with an accurate assessment of a person with a disability. For example, if "is a team player" is not defined by task or responsibility measures, a manager or supervisor could include such factors as whether the employee went to lunch with the team. If, for example, a wheelchair user knew that the restaurant where the team typically went to lunch was not accessible, (s)he might not feel comfortable raising the issue.

3. *Do any of the evaluation factors unnecessarily measure the effects of a disability?* This item logically follows the previous one. The evaluation criteria could be worded in such a way as to shift the weight of the evaluation directly onto disability-related factors. For example, the essential function of "provide weekly project status reports at staff meetings" could be evaluated on the basis of objective criteria, such as on-time submission, correct information, and organization. If, however, an evaluation criterion focused on whether the reports were "effectively communicated," there could be disability-related reasons to lower the score. Consider the case of an employee with a speech impairment, or a situation in which negative, prejudicial attitudes from co-workers created an unpleasant environment and affected the reception of the reports.

4. *Has the evaluation form been reviewed by the employee with a disability to identify any potentially discriminatory criteria?* This activity follows the "win-win" ideal by allowing the employee to provide feedback *before* being evaluated using the form. The organization does not benefit from an inappropriately negative evaluation, and, of course, the individual has much at stake.

5. *Is there any evidence that the person conducting the evaluation*

holds negative views of the employee that are related to the employee's disability? There is no difference between this concern and the kinds of concerns that have been expressed regarding racism, sexism, and ageism. This area is rather new, but that fact reinforces the need for disability awareness training for *all* staff throughout the organization.

EMPLOYMENT ACTIONS

Under the ADA, every employment action should be conducted equitably for people with disabilities. In other words, there should be no double standards, either for or against people with disabilities, except for reasonable accommodations. In this time of transition toward full integration of the ADA, avoiding a double standard may present one of the greatest challenges.

Promotion and Recognition of Outstanding Work

Companies with a "true north" orientation will ensure that people with disabilities are rewarded for excellent performance in the same way and on the same basis as other employees. As noted in the discussion of performance evaluations, the criteria for evaluating performance need to be objective and perform-ance-based. This becomes the foundation for nondiscrimination in promotion and recognition.

But the process of performance recognition can become complicated for people with disabilities, in at least two ways. First, many companies, including some of the "best" we have mentioned, offer awards for "outstanding disabled employee" (or a similar title). This practice may not continue for long, in that it seems to counter the ADA by setting up a separate performance criterion for this group. We are, however, still in the transition phase toward full equality. Thus, the practice may be useful for the time being, as a way to motivate and recognize outstanding performance. It will be crucial to monitor such awards. Under no circumstances should they *replace* bonuses, promotions, and other rewards offered to employees.

The second, more subtle (and even more problematic) issue concerns preconceptions about the ability of employees with disabilities to advance to higher positions within the organization. If the principle of nondiscrimination is really working, the person's disability will not matter. Unfortunately, that is not always the case. Supervisors can impose a career ceiling by simply not recognizing the employee's innate potential, or by allowing patronizing attitudes to come into play (e.g., "With his handicap, he must be glad just to have a job."). On the other extreme, the supervisor may fall victim to the "super-crip" syndrome, lavishing the individual with inappropriate praise or assigning excessive responsibility. Organization-wide training can help head off some of these problems.

Transfer

Job transfers, either to a different geographic location or to a new area of responsibility, are a fact of modern organizational life. For most people with disabilities, nothing about their disability will be a factor in the transfer. Just as any employee may find the change exciting or devastating, so it is with people with disabilities.

However, certain other considerations sometimes come into play for people with disabilities. For example:

- If the person is a wheelchair user and requires paratransit services or other accessible transportation, the new site may lack these services or operate on a significantly different schedule.
- For a person with an environmental illness, a new community or even a new facility may seriously increase the effects of the disability.
- An individual with mental illness may be afraid of the change and not want to do it.

In each of these cases, and others like it, the transfer decision should be discussed with the person with the disability in terms of reasonable accommodations that could be made. This interactive process, as discussed earlier, is intended to create the best possible solution for both parties. If the result of the discussion comes down to the worst-case scenario, specifically that the employer *must* transfer the employee and no accommodations are reasonable, the employer has no obligation under the ADA to create a new position for the individual.

Dismissal

As mentioned earlier, more than 40 percent of the complaints received by the EEOC during the early months of the ADA were for alleged wrongful dismissal. While this may be an artifact of the extent to which companies are downsizing, it is still cause for great concern. As all managers know, the decision to terminate or dismiss must be substantiated on the basis of performance. The decision should be made independently of the employee's disability. Human resource managers may wish to be especially vigilant in this regard.

EMPLOYMENT BENEFITS AND PRIVILEGES

The principles of the ADA and good management call for employers to provide many kinds of employment benefits and privileges. The specific issue of employee benefit programs (leave, insurance, etc.) will be discussed in the final chapter. Our focus here is on the less formal aspects of the employment relationship.

Informal benefits and privileges include everything from coat hooks and cafeterias to company newsletters and picnics. The ADA and good management call for people with disabilities to be fully included in all those benefits and privileges.

In order for this to occur, many managers may have to change their ways of thinking. For example:

- Selection of the location for the company picnic may need to include considerations of accessible sites.
- The cafeteria, kitchenette, or coffee preparation area may need some modifications to make them accessible.
- Obstacles near water fountains and elevator doors may need to be removed.
- The usual restaurant for the "team lunch" may need to make some "readily achievable" changes to become more accessible; alternatively, the team may consider other sites.
- Someone may need to sit near a person with a vision impairment to describe the skits at the office party.
- Sign language interpreters may become part of the routine for corporation meetings.

These are a few examples of the kinds of considerations companies are using to ensure that employees with disabilities enjoy all the benefits and privileges of employment. Again, the best companies involve employees in the decisions.

You may want to begin with two steps: (1) find out if any accommodations are needed by current employees with disabilities, and if they are *reasonable* accommodations, start the process of getting these changes made as soon as possible; and (2) conduct a preliminary survey of employment sites to see what changes can be made without significant difficulty or expense.

4

Special Issues

When the ADA was passed, those most intimately involved with its development recognized that neither they nor anyone else had thought of *all* the questions that the ADA would raise—let alone all the answers. Many of the issues raised during these early discussions involved complex and difficult matters that could be resolved only with time and experience. This chapter discusses a few of these areas: problems that the developers of the ADA did not fully anticipate, as well as questions that could be answered only as the ADA unfolded in the real world.

SUBSTANCE ABUSE: DRUGS AND ALCOHOL

A person who formerly engaged in the illegal use of drugs is considered an "individual with a disability" under the ADA—with the emphasis here on *"formerly."* Individuals who are currently using illegal drugs or who abuse prescription drugs are *not* covered by the ADA. The point needs to be emphasized to all managers and staff: The ADA does not require employers to hire or retain substance abusers or "recreational" drug users.

The best practice in the area of drug and alcohol concerns can be stated this way:

Practice # 14

Establish clear policies regarding alcohol and drug use in the workplace and apply them consistently and objectively.

The ADA's "true north" in this area, as in others we have examined, points to the need to prevent discrimination, but without compromising sound management practices and good business sense. Employers may have policies forbidding employees to engage in the use of alcohol and illegal drugs while at work. Regardless of the logic behind the policy—be it for legal reasons, a matter of employee performance, or simply a point of moral principle—such policies are quite acceptable under the ADA and represent good management practice. The ADA essentially says that an individual should not be denied a job simply because the individual has illegally used drugs *at some point in his or her life.*

As an interesting side note to this view, the policy of the National Football League and other professional sports organizations may be improper under the ADA. The NFL's policy limits the number of times an individual may be caught abusing drugs before incurring a "lifetime ban." The ADA, however, seems to suggest that a person can and should be "forgiven" as many times as he or she shows evidence of being truly rehabilitated. The approach of "three strikes and you're out" (to mix a sports metaphor) appears to use an arbitrary standard for determining when a person's history of abuse can become a legitimate factor in an employment action. If the NFL and others continue to use such standards, they will likely need to justify their actions on the basis of a clear business necessity. The argument might be that repeat offenders tarnish the image of professional sports, and that this results in loss of gate receipts or television revenues.

Following are some general guidelines for managers regarding substance abuse in the workplace under the ADA:

- Persons with a history of substance abuse are protected by the ADA, provided they are not still engaged in the illegal use of drugs.

- If an employee or applicant can demonstrate, at the employer's request, that he or she has been successfully rehabilitated and is no longer illegally using drugs, the employer cannot discriminate against this individual.
- An employer may prohibit the illegal use of drugs and the use of alcohol in the workplace and may forbid employees to be under the influence of alcohol or illegally used drugs while at the workplace.
- An employer may also hold all employees to the same performance or conduct standards, regardless of the effect of current or prior substance abuse on an individual employee.
- An employer may fire or refuse to hire someone who is "currently engaging" in the illegal use of drugs; "currently" is not defined by a specified number of days or weeks prior to the employment action, but "recently enough to indicate that the individual is actively engaged in such conduct."
- An employer may require that employees conform to the requirements of the Drug-Free Workplace Act and any other relevant laws and regulations regarding substance abuse.

Several of these points need some elaboration from a management perspective. First, what is meant by "currently" engaged in the illegal use of drugs? This is one area where the legal department could profitably be consulted; the ADA makes it very hard for managers to determine precisely what is meant. The guidance from EEOC says that:

"Current" drug use means that the illegal use of drugs occurred recently enough to justify an employer's reasonable belief that involvement with drugs is an on-going problem. It is not limited to the day of use, or recent weeks or days, in terms of an employment action. It is determined on a case-by-case basis.

In other words, this is clearly a judgment call. This raises, again, the issue of the case-by-case analysis that is central to the

ADA. Managers and supervisors need to learn to apply this concept, but with clear, objective reasons for making the judgment and with on-file documentation explaining how the decision was made.

EEOC goes on to provide an example of how the case-by-case determination might work for someone evidently engaged in "current" illegal use of drugs:

> For example: An applicant or employee who tests positive for an illegal drug cannot immediately enter a drug rehabilitation program and seek to avoid the possibility of discipline or termination by claiming that (s)he now is in rehabilitation and is no longer using drugs illegally. A person who tests positive for illegal use of drugs is not entitled to the protection that may be available to former users who have been or are in rehabilitation now.

The point here is that a person who is a current illegal user of drugs has no protection under the ADA, no matter how creative he or she may be in trying to slip in under the wire. The manager's job, and normally the HR manager's job, is to make the call about the recentness of the use and to decide whether the individual can justifiably be shown to be making good-faith efforts to overcome the problem, such as enrollment in a 28-day rehabilitation program.

On a related note, the science of drug testing, as most HR managers are well aware, is still evolving. Some prescription medications can give a false positive on a drug test. To the extent possible, managers will need to work closely with medical staff as well as with the drug testing organization to ensure that a person is not wrongfully denied an employment opportunity.

The issue of on-the-job performance once again brings us back to a point where the ADA and good management converge. A manager or supervisor may suspect (or even be absolutely sure) that an employee is under the influence of drugs or alcohol on the job. But the manager's action should be directed at the primary concern: performance.

If the person becomes listless or sluggish, or begins to behave strangely or erratically, the cause of the behavior could be any number of things, none of them drug or alcohol related. (The employee may be under personal stress, suffering from an emotional problem, or experiencing side effects from a prescription medication.) The cause is not the issue. Supervisors have a right, for example, to expect employees to come to work on time, unless an exception has been arranged in advance. If an employee is late for work, especially on a regular basis, that *behavior* is unacceptable regardless of the cause. Supervisors should meet with the individual and discuss the problem, attempting to focus on *solutions*. If the problem persists, the supervisor can let the employee know that the behavior will result in a disciplinary action, possibly termination, unless something is done to change it. At that point, the manager may offer the individual an opportunity to talk with a counselor or HR staff person about programs that the organization offers or knows about for counseling, drug treatment, or other needs, including employee assistance programs.

The purpose of this section of the ADA is to support the management goal of hiring and keeping good people, regardless of their history, unless they cannot meet the company's standards of conduct and performance. If they cannot, managers then must do what managers do best: make decisions about whether to try to remedy the problem or terminate the employee. The best companies first make every reasonable attempt to remedy, and terminate only as a last resort.

Drug Testing

On this matter the ADA has again left much to the discretion of managers. The ADA neither promotes nor discourages drug testing. Unlike medical tests, drug tests can be required of applicants before a conditional offer of employment, and the company can make a hiring decision based on a positive test result. The major items to consider related to drug testing under the ADA are:

- The ADA takes a neutral position on drug testing and does not "encourage, prohibit, or authorize" drug testing by employers, leaving the decision on whether or not to test up to the employer.

- The results of drug tests may be used as a basis for disciplinary action by an employer.
- Drug tests are not considered medical examinations under the ADA, but the information from the tests, including medical information not directly related to the use of drugs, must still be treated as a confidential medical record.

The management actions to make this work are to:

- Develop the approach and justification for the corporate employee drug testing policy, and document it.
- Ground the policy in business necessity and other appropriate considerations such as employee health and safety.
- Ensure that the policy is enforced consistently and without discrimination.

The most important aspect of this whole issue of illegal use of drugs is to act consistently and in keeping with sound management principles. Managers who have experienced difficulty in handling this issue may well benefit from some "peer consulting" with HR staff.

WORKERS' COMPENSATION

Employers' costs for workers' compensation have nearly tripled in the past decade, increasing from just over $20 billion in 1980 to more than $60 billion today. In 1980, the average cost per claim was a modest $1,748; in 1990, it had climbed to $6,611. During the same period, the average wage-replacement cost per claim rose from $4,390 to $12,833. These figures have understandably caused employers a great deal of concern.

The ADA has heightened these concerns because of two major misconceptions: (1) that people with disabilities are more likely to make a workers' compensation claim; and (2) that employers will be unable to screen out candidates with a history of workers' compensation claims because it would be discriminatory to do so under the ADA. The reality is that neither of these fears has a strong factual basis.

The belief that people with disabilities will file more workers' compensation claims is based largely on myths and stereotypes. As with all other aspects of the ADA, each case and situation must be handled individually. The ADA permits employers to make informed, objective judgments about whether a person, either because of a disability or other reason, poses a health or safety risk to him/herself or others. According to the EEOC, "The employer must be prepared to show that there is:

- significant risk of substantial harm;
- the specific risk must be identified;
- the assessment of risk must be based on objective medical or other factual evidence regarding a particular individual; and
- even if a genuine significant risk of substantial harm exists, the employer must consider whether the risk can be eliminated or reduced below the level of a "direct threat" by *reasonable accommodation.*"

These elements provide the parameters for an informed management decision about the risk posed by a person with a disability, and about whether there really is a greater likelihood that the individual will make a workers' compensation claim, compared with other employees.

To prevent prejudgments about the risk, employers may not ask a candidate about his/her workers' compensation history prior to a conditional offer of employment, either on the application or in an interview. However, after a conditional offer has been made, questions may be asked about workers' compensation claims history, but only if *all* candidates are asked as part of a medical examination or inquiry. The only circumstance where this information can be used in a hiring decision is when the individual poses a "significant risk of substantial harm" to self or others on the job, as discussed above. In other words, employers cannot deny a person a position simply because they think the individual *may* raise workers' compensation costs in the future.

One statistic that employers probably do not want to hear, but likely know already, comes from EEOC. Of complaints received by EEOC in the first month of the ADA (250), the most frequently cited disability was a back impairment. Employers have feared that "goldbricks" pretending to have injuries, especially back injuries, would try to exploit the ADA. Morale problems sometimes arise when co-workers believe an individual is getting special treatment (e.g., light-duty work) because of a faked condition. Nothing in the ADA can prevent people from faking a disability, but the ADA actually can become a management tool in this respect. Before an individual can make a workers' compensation claim or go on paid leave for a disability, the employer can offer to make a reasonable accommodation that will allow the individual to continue working, but with some modifications. Companies can accommodate the person without creating an incentive to fake an injury.

Actions employers can take under the ADA to help keep workers' compensation costs in line include:

• *Screening out applicants with a history of fraudulent workers' compensation claims.* This is still permissible under the ADA, and necessary for good management.

• *Developing a mechanism or set of procedures to determine when an employee poses a direct threat to the health and safety of her/himself or others.* Using the criteria listed earlier, a form or checklist could be developed. This would help to ensure that the assessment of risk is based on objective medical evidence and not fears, suspicions, or myths, and that the process allows for reasonable accommodations to be attempted to reduce the threat to an acceptable level.

• *Developing a coordinated effort among all appropriate departments within and outside the organization to manage workers' compen-*

sation costs and work-related injuries within ADA guidelines. This includes safety and health officials, state workers' compensation agencies, and others.

Many companies have set these processes in motion already, and simply need to ensure that they do not lead to ungrounded decisions. Again, focusing on good management and the ADA's "true north" reminds us that the goal of this discussion is to avoid preventing a valuable employee from being denied a position for the wrong reasons. If the reasons are valid, such as legitimate health and safety concerns, neither the ADA nor good management will prohibit the employment action. If, on the other hand, the actions lack an objective basis in health and safety concerns, the decision or employment action needs to be considered for other, more appropriate reasons, including productivity.

THE ADA AND THE REHABILITATION ACT

The Rehabilitation Act of 1973 (as amended) provides for nondiscrimination on the basis of disability in all programs and activities that are funded or conducted by the federal government. The language and conceptual approach of *Section 504* of the Rehabilitation Act was the basis for the ADA.

The Rehabilitation Act covers:

- All recipients of federal funds, including state and local governments, most colleges and universities, nonprofit organizations having federal grants, most hospitals and long-term care facilities; and
- All federal government contractors and subcontractors.

Exhibit 4.1 provides a visual representation of the major sections of the Rehabilitation Act and what each covers.

Those businesses and organizations that are covered by the

Exhibit 4.1. What the Rehabilitation Act of 1973 covers.

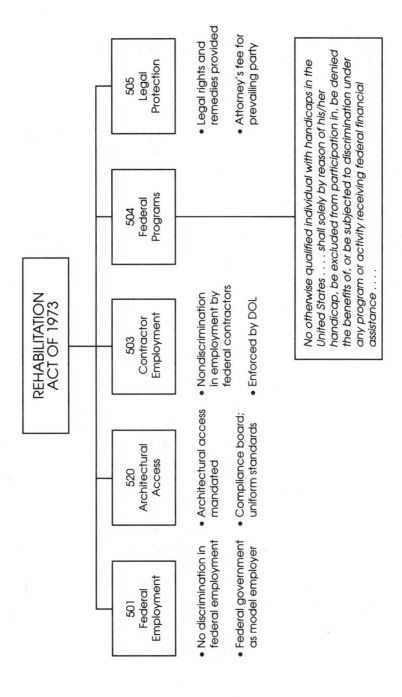

Rehabilitation Act are already required to comply with most of the ADA's provisions. Key points to know:

- The ADA does not substantially change the requirements of *Section 504* for federal funding recipients, but it has strengthened the enforcement of *Section 504*; and
- Federal contractors must continue to abide by the affirmative action requirements of *Section 503* of the Rehabilitation Act, even with the ADA in effect.

Employers covered by the Rehabilitation Act, whether *Section 503* or *504*, should be sure that they are as familiar with it as they are with the ADA. Each federal agency that serves as a funding source for public or private employers has an office designated to provide information and technical assistance on the Rehabilitation Act. For example, hospitals and nursing homes should contact the Department of Health and Human Services; colleges and universities, the Department of Education; and so forth.

Federal Contractors and *Section 503*

As just noted, employers with federal contracts are covered by both the Americans with Disabilities Act and the Rehabilitation Act of 1973. Any company that holds a federal government contract is covered by *Section 503*, which requires not only nondiscrimination but affirmative action in the employment of people with disabilities. While the ADA is not itself an affirmative action law, it does not change the affirmative action requirements of *Section 503* for federal contractors.

Companies that are federal contractors should continue to collect information on disability as part of their affirmative action programs, and may continue to make pre-employment inquiries about disability under the guidelines of the *Section 503* regulations. In this respect, *Section 503* supersedes the ADA. Where, for example, the ADA forbids employers to ask job applicants to identify themselves as having a disability,

Section 503 permits it specifically for affirmative action purposes. The ADA does, however, expand some nondiscrimination requirements for federal contractors, and so should not be ignored.

Because of potential confusion over which law applies to an employment discrimination charge brought against a federal contractor by a person with a disability, EEOC and the Department of Labor's Office of Federal Contract Compliance Programs (OFCCP) have developed an interagency agreement. Disability-related discrimination companies will all be handled in the same way, regardless of whether the charge was initially filed under the ADA or *Section 503*.

HEALTH INSURANCE

The impact of the ADA on employee benefits is not completely clear at this point, to say the least. One key element, health insurance, has been described by many organizations for people with disabilities as the "unfinished business of the ADA." This concern about health insurance for people with disabilities comes at a time when health insurance costs have reached a crisis point and nearly everyone agrees something must be done. The response of business has been to require employees to share in the costs. As an illustration of the extent of the problem, the Employers Council on Flexible Compensation reported that more than half of its members plan to change their benefits plans in 1993, primarily to address problems of high health-care costs.

The ADA does not require employers to provide health plans for its employees, but it does require "equal access" for employees with disabilities to plans that are provided. The ADA also was designed not to "disrupt the current nature of insurance underwriting," including pre-existing conditions clauses. The only exception is when an employer engages in practices that are considered as deliberate "subterfuge" of the ADA's goals. Benefits caps for specific conditions appear to be prohibited by the ADA, but since the ADA does permit limitations on the number of treatments, this issue remains in the gray area.

What this means is that, as of now, the employer can apparently continue to administer health-care plans as usual, but with a close eye on developments of the ADA's impact on health insurance. The best management strategy will include a monitoring system to identify emerging issues in employer-provided health insurance, and an ongoing dialogue with insurance carriers and employees with disabilities. The ADA's first principle of nondiscrimination means that exclusionary health insurance plans are a potentially significant problem; good management under the ADA means that health-care costs and employee productivity will be two key factors in an equation of long-term benefits to the organization and its employees.

Appendix A

Examples of Reasonable Accommodations

The first six examples were provided by TransCen, Inc., of Rockville, Maryland, a firm specializing in effective employment of people with disabilities.

Office Clerk

Primary Duties: Sorting and delivering office mail throughout a large division office. Photocopying and procuring supplies at the supply store.

Employee Characteristics: Employee has spina bifida. He uses both a manual wheelchair and an electric wheelchair for mobility on the job. He drives his own adapted car.

Accommodations: The mailboxes into which he sorts mail were lowered to arm reach from his wheelchair. At work, he substitutes the use of his manual wheelchair with his electric wheelchair, both of which he owned prior to his employment. A wire mesh basket was added to his electric wheelchair, thus enabling him to deliver the various mail and photocopy items from floor to floor throughout the building. Furniture and

boxes were removed from his path to allow for wider wheel-chair access. A short wooden dowel gives him the added arm reach he sometimes needs to engage rear photocopy buttons.
Cost to Employer: Less than $150.

Food Preparation Worker

Primary Duties: Preparing and mixing pizza dough at a large national franchise restaurant, placing the dough in the oven to "proof," and adding the pizza sauce.

Employee Characteristics: Employee is moderately mentally re-tarded and visually impaired.

Accommodations: To accommodate her visual impairment, a thick line of dark indelible ink was marked on the measuring cup at the level to which the cup needs to be filled. An indelible ink mark also has been made on the oven dial to enable her to see where to set the dial for correct temperatures. Initial on-the-job training was provided by her job coach, employed by a local rehabilitation agency.

Cost to Employer: $0.

Sales Associate

Primary Duties: Initiating customer contact via telephone and written correspondence, answering customer inquiries or-ders, and tabulating daily quotas.

Employee Characteristics: Employee has quadriplegia. He uses a wheelchair for mobility and requires typing splints for his fingers to compensate for limited digital dexterity. He has a bachelor's degree in business administration.

Accommodations: His desk was raised with wood blocks to allow for space for the wheelchair to fit under. A small attachment to the telephone receiver allows easier handling of the tele-phone. A slightly "flexed" schedule eases transportation and attendant care arrangements.

Cost to Employer: $40 for the telephone attachment and wood blocks.

Assistant Store Manager

Primary Duties: Assisting the manager, tracking convenience store inventory, ordering the necessary items, overseeing the vending of hot food, operating the cash register when necessary, and supervising part-time store clerks.

Employee Characteristics: Employee has specific learning disabilities, including dyslexia.

Accommodations: Since the employee had worked as a full-time clerk for over a year, he knew all aspects of his job well. Due to his reading difficulties, however, he was unable to pass the written exam needed for promotion to assistant store manager in the standard allotment of time. The company arranged for the exam monitor to read him the questions so that he could respond more quickly. After scoring one of the highest marks ever achieved on the test, he was immediately promoted to assistant store manager.

Cost to Employer: $0.

Receptionist

Primary Duties: Interacting with the public entering a busy university office. Responding to requests for transcripts, schedules, registration, and grade inquiries.

Employee Characteristics: Employee uses a wheelchair for mobility and has limited arm reach.

Accommodations: To allow the employee to reach the computer keyboard used to answer student requests, a semi-circle was cut out of the front receptionist counter, enabling the employee to be closer to the keyboard and to better access the counter space without having to move her wheelchair.

Cost to Employer: $200 for carpentry work.

Stock Clerk

Primary Duties: Stocking and cleaning the showroom of a large retail store.

Employee Characteristics: Employee has a learning disability that makes it difficult for her to process oral directions.

Accommodations: A chart was posted in a convenient location, listing the sequence of duties. This list is organized on a daily basis with a specified time allotment for each task. The list provides the employee with the structure to move independently from one job function to the next, and has actually decreased the amount of supervisory time needed.

Cost to Employer: $0.

EXAMPLES OF EQUIPMENT MODIFICATIONS OR DEVICES

The EEOC has given the following examples of ways in which an employer could reasonably accommodate an individual with a disability by modifying standard equipment:

- A telephone amplifier designed to work with a hearing aid allowed a plant worker to retain his job and avoid transfer to a lower paying job. Cost: $24;
- A blind receptionist was provided a light probe that allowed her to determine which lines on the switchboard were ringing, on hold, or in use. (A light probe gives an audible signal when held over an illuminated source.) Cost: $50–$100;
- A person working in the food service position, who had use of only one hand, could perform all tasks except opening cans. She was provided with an electric can opener. Cost: $35;
- Purchase of a lightweight mop and a smaller broom enabled an employee with Down's syndrome and congenital heart problems to do his job with minimal strain. Cost: under $40;
- A truck driver had carpal tunnel syndrome which limited his wrist movement and caused extreme discomfort in cold weather. A special wrist splint used with a glove designed for skin divers made it possible for him to drive even in extreme weather conditions. Cost: $55;

- A phone headset allowed an insurance salesman with cerebral palsy to write while talking to clients. Rental cost: $6 per month;
- A simple cardboard form, called a "jog," made it possible for a person with mental retardation to properly fold jeans as a stock clerk in a retail store. Cost: $0;
- A timer with an indicator light allowed a medical technician who was deaf to perform laboratory tests. Cost: $27;
- A clerk with limited use of her hands was provided a "lazy susan" file holder that enabled her to reach all materials needed for her job. Cost: $85;
- A groundskeeper who had limited use of one arm was provided a detachable extension arm for a rake. This enabled him to grasp the handle on the extension with the impaired hand and control the rake with the functional arm. Cost: $20;
- A desk layout was changed from the right to the left side to enable a data entry operator who is visually impaired to perform her job. Cost: $0.

OTHER EXAMPLES

A major insurance company reports these accommodations:

- Providing a drafting table, page turner, and pressure-sensitive tape recorder for a sales agent paralyzed from a broken neck ($300).
- Supplying a telephone amplifier for a computer programmer with a hearing impairment ($56).
- Enlarging toilet facilities and installing a hand rail for employees who use wheelchairs ($500).
- Removing turnstiles in the cafeteria and installing lighter weight doors—as part of a general renovation—and having the cafeteria deliver lunch to a payroll technician disabled from polio ($40 per month).
- Providing a special chair to alleviate back pain for a district sales agent affected by vertebra surgery ($400).

Appendix B

Reasonable Accommodations for People with Psychiatric Disabilities

By Jacqueline Parrish, Director, Community Support Program, National Institute of Mental Health, and Laura Mancuso, Director of Technical Assistance, National Association of State Mental Health Program Directors.

Following is a list of reasonable accommodations that individuals with psychiatric disabilities involved in the Community Support Program demonstration projects, self-help programs, and supported employment services have found helpful.

Human Assistance

Just as a sign language interpreter or personal care attendant might be provided for a person with a hearing impairment or a physical disability, people with psychiatric disabilities may benefit from the provision of human assistance, such as:

- A job coach to help a worker apply interpersonal or time management skills on the job;
- Additional individualized training on specific job tasks or methods;
- Designation of a co-worker to serve as a peer support and/or advocate through regularly scheduled appointments or as needed; and
- Pairing workers with mentors (who may or may not have a disability).

Changes in Workplace Policies

Flexibility in enforcing traditional policies can create helpful, relatively inexpensive accommodations such as:

- Permitting telephone calls during work hours to friends or other supportive individuals;
- Allowing people to work at home;
- Allowing use of sick leave for emotional as well as physical illness; and
- Reserving an enclosed office for an entry-level worker who loses concentration and accuracy amid distractions.

Because of the episodic nature of mental disorders, flexible scheduling can be an essential accommodation for individuals with psychiatric disabilities. Specific strategies include the following:

- Allowing workers to shift work hours for medical appointments or emotional needs;
- Advancing additional paid or unpaid leave during a hospitalization;
- Creating a job-sharing policy;

- Keeping a job open and/or providing backup coverage during a period of extended leave; and
- Permitting a self-paced workload.

Supervision

Good supervision improves anyone's work situation, but it may be critical to the success of workers with psychiatric disabilities. Supervisory accommodations include the following:

- Assigning or reassigning the worker to a supervisor who is supportive and has good listening skills;
- Offering management training to all supervisors to improve their ability to provide clear direction and constructive feedback;
- Educating managers about the ADA so they can have frank discussions with applicants and/or workers about known disabilities and desirable accommodations;
- Training supervisors to offer praise and positive reinforcement;
- Instructing supervisors to provide detailed explanations of job duties, responsibilities, and expectations; and
- Establishing written agreements between workers and supervisors for short-term performance indicators, work flow management, and handling crises.

Shaping Co-workers' Attitudes

Proactive strategies for making a workplace "emotionally accessible" include the following:

- Sensitivity training for co-workers about disabilities;
- Staging open discussions involving disabled and non-disabled workers to air feelings;
- Orienting co-workers as to why people with disabilities receive accommodations; and

---

A Quick Look at How Title I of the ADA Protects People with Psychiatric Disabilities

It is now illegal for employers to:

- Ask job applicants about psychiatric treatment—past or present;
- Deny a job to someone with the necessary experience and skills because of the person's past or current psychiatric treatment or possible future treatment;
- Deny a job or promotion because of a belief that a person with a mental disability won't be able to "handle" the job;
- Refuse to make reasonable modifications in workplace rules, schedules, policies, or procedures that would help a person with a mental disability perform the job;
- Force an employee with mental disabilities to accept a workplace modification;
- Contract with other organizations and individuals that discriminate against people with mental disabilities; or
- Retaliate against people with mental disabilities for asserting their rights.

- Dispelling myths by educating staff about the causes, treatment, and personal experience of mental illness.

Guiding Principles for Providing Reasonable Accommodations

Providing reasonable accommodations in a manner that empowers rather than stigmatizes the individual includes the following:

- Recognizing the individual's strengths and potential contributions to the organization;
- Being willing to engage in joint problem-solving;

- Involving the individual in all decision making related to restructuring a job and developing reasonable accommodations;
- Making only voluntary reasonable accommodations; and
- Providing an environment in which disclosure is not punished, but conversely the individual's desire for confidentiality is respected.

Appendix C

ADA Tax Credit Provisions

PROVISIONS OF *SECTION 44*

Under *Section 44,* an eligible small business may elect to take a general business credit of up to $5,000 annually for eligible access expenditures to comply with the requirements of the Americans with Disabilities Act. The amount that may be taken as a credit is 50% of the eligible access expenditures incurred that exceed $250 but do not exceed $10,250 per tax year. For instance, if an expenditure of $7,500 is made for the provision of an interpreter, the credit would be in the amount of $3,625 ($7,500 minus $250 divided by 2). The credit can be carried forward up to 15 years and carried back for three years, though there is no carryback to a year before 1990. A business may take this credit each year that it makes an accessibility expenditure, be it purchase of equipment, provision of communication assistance or removal of an architectural barrier. This tax credit will be claimed on IRS Form 8826, *Disabled Access Credit.*

Source: Paralyzed Veterans of America brochure, "Tax Incentives: Assisting Accessibility."

Definitions of Major Terms for *Section 44*

Eligible Small Business: A business with gross receipts of no more than $1 million or 30 or fewer full-time (30 hours a week for 20 or more weeks a year) employees for the year preceding the taxable year.

Eligible Access Expenditures: Reasonable expenditures to comply with the ADA. Included are amounts related to removing architectural, communication, physical or transportation barriers; providing qualified interpreters, readers or similar services; modifying or acquiring equipment and materials. Expenditures must be reasonable and meet standards set out in the regulations issued by the IRS; however, these regulations have not yet been published. Expenses for new construction or those that are not necessary to accomplish ADA accessibility are *not* eligible.

PROVISIONS OF *SECTION 190*

All businesses may elect to treat qualified architectural and transportation barrier removal expenses that are paid or incurred during each taxable year as expenses that are not chargeable to a capital account. Such expenditures are to be fully deductible up to a maximum of $15,000 for each taxable year. Qualified expenses include only those expenses specifically attributable to the removal of existing barriers such as steps, narrow doors, inaccessible parking spaces; inaccessible toilet facilities or transportation vehicles. For instance, if a restaurant spends $12,000 installing ramps, re-striping the parking lot and widening passageways, the full $12,000 is deductible. Modifications must meet the requirements of standards established under *Section 190* of the Internal Revenue Code *(26CFR Section 1.190)*. Expenses incurred in the construction or comprehensive renovation of a facility or vehicle or the normal replacement of depreciable property are not included.

AVAILABILITY

Section 44 and *Section 190* may be taken on an annual basis. A business that cannot remove all barriers in one year or provide accommodations on a continuing basis may use these incentives each year that an eligible expenditure is made.

Appendix D

Resources

FEDERAL GOVERNMENT ADA TECHNICAL ASSISTANCE RESOURCES

Equal Employment Opportunity Commission

ADA Helpline (800) 669-EEOC (voice) or (800) 800-3302
(TDD) ADA Technical Assistance Manual and other
informational booklets are available.

Regional Disability and Business Technical Assistance Centers

Toll-free telephone number for all 10 centers: (800) 949-
4232 (automatically connects to the appropriate regional
center)

Job Accommodation Network

(800) 526-7234 for accommodation information (out of
West Virginia)
(800) 526-4698 for accommodation information (West
Virginia only)

(800) ADA WORK (800) 232-9675 ADA information (voice/ TDD)
(800) DIAL JAN (800) 342-5526 ADA information (computer modem)

ADA-RELATED MATERIALS AVAILABLE FROM THE NATIONAL EASTER SEAL SOCIETY

Call: (312) 726-6200 (voice) or (312) 726-4258 (TDD)

Attitude Awareness

Brochures
Tips for Disability Awareness
Tips for Portraying People with Disabilities in the Media

Video Cassettes
Party
Wheelchair

Audio Cassettes
Sticks and Stones
Unfriendly Skies
I'm Not Prejudiced

Posters and Post Cards
Awareness is the First Step Towards Change

Employers

Books and Brochures
Americans with Disabilities Act: An Easy Checklist for Business
The Workplace Workbook: An Illustrated Guide to Job Accommodation and Assistive Technology
Building Bridges—Access to America's Hot New Market

Video Cassettes
Part of the Team
Nobody is Burning Wheelchairs

Legislation

Brochures
The Americans with Disabilities Act
The Air Carrier Access Act

Video Cassettes
Pizza

Audio Cassettes
Americans with Disabilities Act
Pizza

Posters and Post Cards
It Took an Act of Congress

Transportation

Books and Brochures
Project ACTION
Project ACTION's Combined Research Findings
Project ACTION's Reconnaissance Survey

Video Cassettes
Providing Public Transportation to Everyone
Bus

Audio Cassettes
Project ACTION
Trains

Posters and Post Cards
Because Public Transportation is for Everyone

About the Author

Timothy L. Jones is president of Fourth Sector Management, Inc., a management consulting firm specializing in the application of effective management to the processes of implementing public policy. His federal government clients have included the Departments of Energy, Defense, Veterans Affairs, and Housing and Urban Development, as well as the National Council on Disability. While associate vice president of client affairs at The Naisbitt Group, he consulted for major corporations, including General Motors, IBM, Campbell Soup, ARCO, Coors, General Foods, and Merrill Lynch.

Mr. Jones's work on the ADA includes directing a federally funded national study of the progress and issues of ADA implementation, a project covering all parts of the ADA and all economic sectors. He has also published articles on the ADA and conducted training seminars focusing on practical, cost-effective management strategies for complying with the ADA's employment provisions.

Mr. Jones has extensive experience in disability-related management and research projects preceding the ADA. He has written numerous training and technical-assistance manuals on *Section 504* of the Rehabilitation Act, the model legislation for the ADA, and has assisted federal funding recipients with *Section 504* implementation. In addition, he has served as project director on several national and regional surveys of persons with disabilities, studies that incorporated a total of over 15,000 interviews.

FOR ADDITIONAL COPIES OF THIS BRIEFING

Additional copies of *The Americans with Disabilities Act: A Review of Best Practices* can be ordered by calling 1-800-538-4761, or by writing to AMA Publication Services, P.O. Box 319, Saranac Lake, NY 12983. $10 per single copy; substantial discounts on bulk orders (11 or more copies). Ask for stock #02350.

OTHER RECENT PUBLICATIONS IN THE MANAGEMENT BRIEFING SERIES

Blueprints for Service Quality: The Federal Express Approach

> Detailed information on the policies and programs that were instrumental in helping Federal Express win the 1990 Malcolm Baldrige National Quality Award. Stock #02347. $10.00

Next Operation as Customer, by Keki Bhote

> How to evaluate and improve internal customer processes—based on a program the author implemented at Motorola. Stock #02346. $12.00

Quality Alone Is Not Enough, by Philip Thomas, Larry Gallace, and Kenneth R. Martin.

> How cycle time management and process simplification can lower costs and improve quality. Stock #2349. $10.00